The
Complete Guide to
PICTURE
FRAMING

Techniques ◆ *Materials*

The
Complete Guide to
PICTURE
FRAMING

Techniques ◆ *Materials*

JENNY RODWELL & GEORGE SHORT

Macdonald

A Macdonald Book
Copyright © Quarto Publishing Ltd 1986

First published in Great Britain in 1986
Published by Macdonald & Co (Publishers) Ltd
London & Sydney
A member of BPCC plc

British Library Cataloguing in Publication Data
Rodwell, Jenny
   The complete guide to picture framing.
   1. Picture frames and framing
   I. Title   II. Short, George
   749'.7   N8550

   ISBN 0-356-12376-6

This book was designed and produced by
Quarto Publishing Ltd
The Old Brewery, 6 Blundell Street
London N7 9BH

Senior editor: Jane Laing
Art editor: Moira Clinch
Editorial: Polly Powell, Michelle Newton
Designer: Rita Wuthrich
Design assistants: Anthony Bussey, Fraser Newman,
Ursula Dawson
Illustrators: Ray Brown, Fraser Newman, Mick Hill
Photographers: Mac Campeanu, John Heseltine
Consultants: Peter Worley and staff at the Newgate
Gallery, London, Christine Ovel, Aidan Walker
Indexer: Richard Bird

Art director: Nigel Osborne
Editorial director: Jim Miles

Typeset by Facsimile Graphics Ltd, Coggeshall
Paste-up by Elly King, Dave Evans
Colour origination by Rainbow Graphic Arts Co Ltd,
Hong Kong
Printed by Lee Fung Asco Printers Ltd, Hong Kong

Macdonald & Co (Publishers) Ltd
Maxwell House
74 Worship Street
London EC2A 2EN

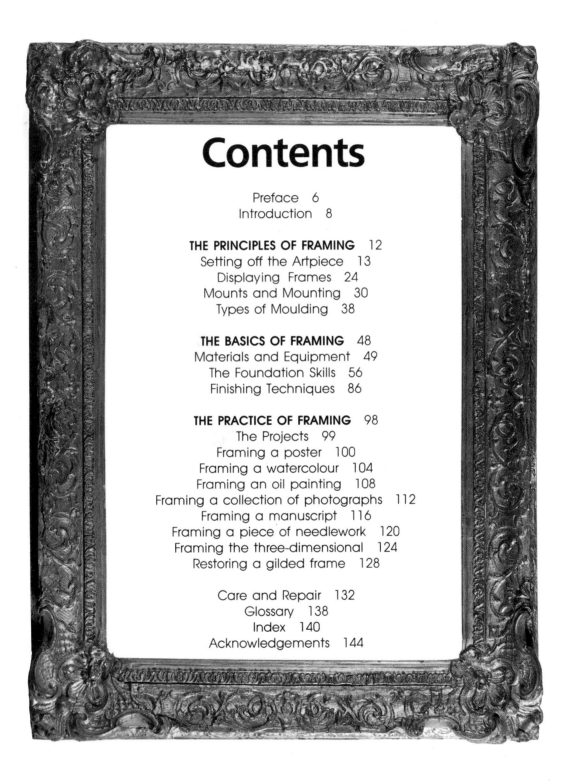

Contents

Preface

Whether a gilded border of ornate decorations or a simple band of metal, the frame plays a major role in the total visual impact of an artpiece, enhancing or seriously distorting the overall effect of the image. The most suitable choice is not always the most obvious one and this book offers valuable guidelines on selecting frames for a wide variety of artpieces, including the three-dimensional. In many cases you will be unable to find a perfectly suitable ready-made frame and will want to make your own. The *Complete Guide to Picture Framing* tells you how.

The basic principles and techniques of framing and mounting are clearly explained and step-by-step illustrated instructions guide you through all the foundation skills of picture framing, from measuring the artpiece to giving your frames a special finish. A large project section, covering a wide range of framing techniques, will enable you to complete different types of frame for different types of artwork. There is a section on the tools and materials needed — it always pays to buy the best you can afford; cheap tools can let you down badly — and a section on the care and repair of both frames and artworks, which will prove especially useful to all those interested in buying second-hand frames and tailoring them to their own requirements. Many damaged frames can be successfully renovated and even the oldest picture frames can usually be stripped of plaster and gilt and the wooden base used as the foundation for one of your own finishes.

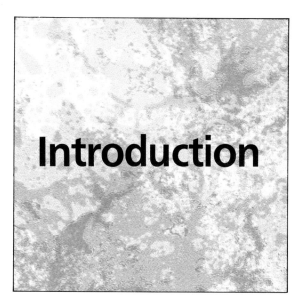

Introduction

Although there have been some spectacular exceptions, such as the ancient cave paintings and some murals, a frame is normally needed to act as a boundary. It therefore plays an important role in the composition of a picture. A church steeple in a landscape painting, for instance, will often be slightly offset, rather than centred, to give a more interesting composition but this is effective only if the limits to the picture are obvious. For, without limits, the whole idea of a composition becomes meaningless and the shapes in the picture merge into the surroundings.

The frame also prevents the 'escape' of colours from an artpiece into the surrounding room. A block of colour in a picture will 'jump out' if there is a similar colour nearby and the picture is not framed. The frame defines the extent of the artpiece and stops this subconscious action of the human eye. It plays exactly the same role in preventing the surface of a picture from becoming merged and confused with the surrounding surface, such as a patterned wallpaper.

On a more practical level, the frame protects the artwork from damage. It guards against general wear and tear and against accident when an artwork is being handled.

THE DEVELOPMENT OF FRAMING

In the ancient classical world, frames were made mainly for mirrors. The Romans and Greeks painted frescos directly onto walls without frames as they are now known. Meanwhile, the Oriental civilizations were developing their own distinct attitude towards paintings. Chinese and Japanese artists painted their works upon folding screens, which divided rooms, and scrolls, which were hung directly on the wall without frames.

In Medieval times, artists began painting onto the slightly hollowed surface of wooden panels and the raised edges, often decorated with separate motifs, gradually developed into a formal picture frame. To begin with frames were frequently part of the solid piece, rather than existing in their own right, and the first separate frames were imitations of their original architectural surroundings — an environment which

The emerging frame
Rich bands of intricate decoration surround these paintings of the early Renaissance. The setting, like the picture itself, was inspired by religion and given up to the glory of God. Intricate patterns (left) are worked around the Lamentation over the Body of Christ *by Giotto. The triptych* Madonna and Child *by Duccio (above) is an altarpiece painted into hinged, recessed panels which are the forerunners of the modern frame.*

Imitating architecture
Attempts to imitate architectural designs led to the creation of styles which gradually evolved into the modern frame. On each side of the Baptism *by della Francesca (left) stand two pilasters, fake 'pillars', such as would be found on a doorway or impressive window recess.*

The simple, sombre frame surrounding Blake's watercolour on wood, The Body of Abel Found by Adam and Eve *(above), highlights the dramatic nature of the painting.*

The contemporary artist, Howard Hodgkin, has incorporated the frame into his oil painting on wood, D H in Hollywood *(right) to vivid and complementary effect.*

was ornate and ecclesiastical. As cathedrals and larger churches were built they demanded even grander architecture. The frame, like the architecture, became more elaborate, as can be seen in the lavish arches, pinnacles and carvings around the Polyptych altarpiece in the Strozzi Chapel, Santa Maria Novella, Florence, by Andrea Orcagna (*c.* 1308–1368). One style which became popular was the Tabernacle frame, a literal imitation of a window recess in which pilasters, make-believe 'pillars' or flattened versions of columns, flanked the painting. The *Madonna and Child with Saints and Donors* in Santo Spirito, Florence, by Filippino Lippi (*c.* 1457–1504), provides an outstanding example of such a Tabernacle frame.

The real breakthrough for the picture frame came in the late fifteenth and early sixteenth centuries when painters began to see themselves as artists in their own right and not simply as servants of architects. They required frames to set their paintings apart from their surroundings. Some of the best frames ever made date from this period. One of the new styles to evolve was the Tondo or circular type exemplified by the intricately carved, wide, gilded frame surrounding the *Holy Family* by Michelangelo, to be found in the Uffizi Gallery in Florence.

Sixteenth-century frame makers began moving towards a more restrained style and the frame gradually became more harmonious with the picture within. Soon, the wealthier classes began seeking paintings for their own homes. Art was no longer merely for public display and it became a product which increasingly needed to be transported after being bought by an individual; and so picture frames became a practical necessity.

As painters became more in demand, they found they had little time to make their own frames. They passed the work on to their apprentices and to outside specialists and so frame making became a skilled craft with its own separate place in the art industry. Increasingly the frame became the property of the cabinet maker and it changed in style as the style of furniture changed. Materials became more sophisticated; in Puritan-influenced northern Europe exotic woods replaced gaudy gilded mouldings.

From time to time conflicts arose between the painter and the frame maker. In the sixteenth century, for instance, frame makers tried to outdo each other and the frames often outshone the paintings, placing them in settings which were extremely elaborate and often inlaid with materials such as jewels, mother of pearl and ivory. The rich rococo style of architecture and interior decoration, popular in early eighteenth-century France, was reflected in frames, and, although a simpler fashion was intro-

duced with the neoclassical revival in Europe in the late part of that century, the rococo designs kept returning. One of these styles, popular for many years, was the Lawrence frame, named after Sir Thomas Lawrence (1769–1830), a fashionable British portrait painter.

With the growth of Modernism in the early twentieth century, frames were widely denounced as over-elaborate and unnecessary visual competition for the picture. Artists increasingly chose simple frames. Some disregarded the traditional restrictions of the frame, such as the American abstract expressionist, Jackson Pollock (1912–1956), who painted huge canvases of dripping and spattered colours, creating an overall image and generating an energy which many argued would have been inappropriate if contained in a fixed wall-piece. Supporters of this idea talked of a 'visual splash' of colour and shape, which, they argued, did not fit into the conventions of pictorial composition and therefore did not require a frame. During the same period, some museums removed more ornate frames from recent paintings and replaced them with simple ones.

In more recent years, however, there has been a definite revival of interest in, and respect for, the frame. There has also been a rise in the popularity of elaborate frames. Critics report that a number of

artists have turned to the frame for its ability to enhance and even interact with the painted surface. Several contemporary artists have fitted frames specially designed to interact with their pictures. For example, two modern American painters, the abstract artist Marsden Hartley and the figurative painter Maurice Prendergast, sometimes make their own frames to accord with their images and Georgia O'Keefe, another American artist, has solid metal frames specially made to complement her work.

Altering or abandoning the frame is not a new idea. During the Baroque period, which began in Europe in the early seventeenth century, many paintings were reframed in a more ornate style. The gold leaf of some of the new frames introduced to the Pitti Palace in Florence, for instance, was so bright that some said it distracted seriously from the paintings. In the early nineteenth century, Napoleon had many paintings in the Louvre reframed in the then fashionable Empire style.

The picture frame has endured throughout all these changes in fashion and looks set to continue indefinitely as the necessary boundary for most works of art. It has also increasingly come into its own among browsers of stalls and antique shops who wish to frame collections of old prints, maps, posters and other memorabilia.

The Principles of Framing

Setting off the Artpiece
■
Displaying Frames
■
Mounts and Mounting
■
Types of Moulding

Setting off the artpiece

There is really no such thing as the 'right' frame for an artpiece — one correct frame which must belong to a particular image. A vast choice is open to the collector or framer and in the end the choice of frame is a matter of personal taste, which is why this is such a fascinating subject, appealing to the individualist.

There are some principles, however, which can be followed to advantage. They fall into two basic categories: the general and the specific. Different types of frames should be used for different types of artwork — oils, watercolours, posters, photographs and so on; and a frame should be chosen that enhances the individual characteristics of a particular artwork. In all cases, the artwork should dictate the frame and not vice versa. The style and colour of the frame and mount should not fight the artwork for attention, nor should they detract from the image. Rather they should complement the image, drawing attention to it. The viewer should not notice the frame or mount rather than the artwork.

There is a further interesting demarcation between old and new frames. An old frame is not necessarily the best choice for an old artpiece, nor a new frame for a new one. It is a question of style. You may decide that a new artpiece needs an antique-looking frame and, conversely, many old artworks, especially old photographs, look attractive in modern frames. Within these categories there is much scope for imagination. For instance, if you decide on an old-style frame, you are not confined to a genuinely antique one. There are many modern reproduction frames, and reproduction mouldings can be bought and used to make your own 'antiqued' version.

A host of ready-made new frames can also be purchased. The drawback here is the range of sizes available. Pictures, old prints, maps and any other items you may wish to frame do not fall easily into rigid categories of size and shape. You need specific proportions and this should be dictated by the artpiece rather than by the size of frame that happens to be available in a shop.

For some projects, ready-made equipment — such as clip frames or other simple Perspex framing kits — can be useful. Generally speaking, though, you may find this too limiting as your interest grows. Kits for self-assembly frames are available in plastic, metal or wood but, again, the problem is the severely limited range of sizes and styles.

One alternative to buying new frames is to turn to the bargain or junk market. Here you may find a greater range of sizes and styles, often at reasonable prices, because they are frequently damaged.

No matter what kind of frame you decide on, one factor becomes increasingly important as you gain in expertise. This is the need to match the frame to the subject being framed. This section takes a look at the wide variety of artpieces you might wish to frame and offers general guidelines on the most suitable kinds of frames, mounts and finishes. For a more detailed discussion on mounts and mounting, and mouldings see pages 30–37 and 38–47. Details on specific picture framing techniques are given on pages 56–85.

OILS AND ACRYLICS

Pictures in oils or acrylics are usually painted onto canvas stretchers (the canvas stretched taut over a framework of wooden slats), canvas-covered boards, or hardboard. With the stretcher, a traditional surface for oils, extra care has to be taken when framing because the painting is often slightly asymmetrical, the thickness of the canvas varies round the edge, and the slats can cause problems.

As a general rule, paintings in oils or acrylics are not glazed — that is, they are not covered by glass — although sometimes glass is used to provide protection, especially with smaller paintings, when it may also actively enhance the picture.

Oil and acrylic paintings usually have a vigorous presence. There are exceptions but, broadly speaking, the very nature of oil and acrylic paints gives a texture that makes the painting stand out more boldly than would a watercolour or print, especially when the artist has used them in a thick or impastoed manner. When framing most oil paintings, therefore, you are dealing with something which is in relief, literally 'standing out from the wall'.

It is this that governs your choice of frame; it also helps to broaden the choice. You can sometimes make do with narrow batten frames, such as wooden or metal strips, that do not cover any of the surface of the painting but are merely tacked onto the edge of the stretcher. This is a suitable approach if the painting is strong enough to stand out on its own and a slim boundary will suffice.

On the other hand, a strong painting can also take a strong frame. This is especially useful in the case of a small painting. The presence here of a

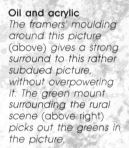

Oil and acrylic
The framers' moulding around this picture (above) gives a strong surround to this rather subdued picture, without overpowering it. The green mount surrounding the rural scene (above right) picks out the greens in the picture.

The polished wooden frame gives it a solid and permanent look. The garden scene (right) is thickly painted with bold colours, using a lot of greens, and the renovated wooden frame complements these textures and colours.

wider frame will help to focus the eye onto the painting itself, which, although small in size, will still be bold enough not to be dominated by the frame. With larger paintings, the freedom of choice is total. They can stand up to 'rougher' stylistic treatment.

WATERCOLOURS

Unlike oils and acrylics, watercolours can suffer terribly from their frames. Generally, watercolours have delicate, washy surfaces and all too often one sees a thinly painted watercolour languishing inside an intricate or heavy frame that makes the picture look as if it is fading away.

By tradition, watercolour frames have been rather unadventurous. They tend to have a subdued look, reflecting the muted tones of the picture they contain. The rugged moorlands or soft trees mellowly depicted by a typical watercolourist like John Sell

Cotman (1782–1842) hang on many walls inside frames which are necessarily low key, with a yellowing, dusty look. This quiet framing style is suited to older watercolours — unfortunately, it has become a tradition for *all* types of watercolours. Some modern pictures, however, deserve a brighter context; the concentrated, luminous colours which many modern watercolourists use can stand up to a more vibrant frame.

Nearly all watercolours stand behind a 'mount', a cardboard 'frame' within the actual frame. This creates a broad expanse of space, providing a sympathetic surround that separates the image from the hard edge of the frame. Since watercolour paints are transparent, they give a fragile, ethereal image and it is generally not a good idea to surround them with an opaque or densely coloured mount. This explains why traditional watercolour

Watercolours
A soft watercolour of Durham Town is given a sympathetic dark brown mount in a gold, antiqued frame (above). The bevelled edge of the mount is lined with antique gold to match the gold on the frame. A large frame with a simple moulding surrounds a cream mount for this small watercolour (left).

mounts are white, cream or pastel-coloured. Again, there are exceptions but these are best done consciously — if you use a bright or dark mount, choose it for a specific reason.

Glass is nearly always used to cover watercolour pictures, as they are far less durable than oils or acrylics. Dust is a great enemy of watercolours, making them dull and dark. Moisture wrinkles the paper and, in extreme conditions, causes the spots of brown mildew known as 'foxing', which can be seen on many older prints and watercolours.

Although the mount is often a broad border around the picture — and the smaller the picture, the bigger the mount can be in contrast — the frame itself should be narrow. Visually, it should make as little fuss as possible, so as not to detract from the picture.

A common characteristic of watercolours is that the paint is rarely taken right up to the edge of the paper. This gives the framer the choice of leaving this unpainted area showing or cropping it closely. Usually, watercolours are best left with the 'random edge' uncropped because this enables the viewer to see how the washes of paint are affected by the paper and the picture benefits from the irregular expanse around its composition.

PASTELS

Pastel paintings, like watercolours, are usually framed by a mount and a frame, and the advice given for mounting and framing watercolours *(see page 14)* applies equally well to pastels.

Pastels are fine chalks and smudge easily. Therefore, in addition to fixing the painting with a fixative spray, a double mount is often used to keep the pastel away from the glass.

PHOTOGRAPHS

Old sepia photographs, popular with collectors, can be greatly enhanced by being framed in traditional style, in keeping with their nostaligic appearance. However, you can use a modern mount and frame to good effect with some images.

With modern photographs, you can rarely afford to take such liberties. Most modern photographs belong firmly to their own era and usually demand a modern frame.

Some framers like to trim off the white edges round photographs but this is not advisable when dealing with the older ones, as the edges often contain fascinating signatures, or captions scribbled in faded ink, or fancy edging reflecting bygone fashions. These characteristics deserve to be preserved and they can be included in the visual whole of the frame. Treatment similar to that of a watercolour is best here: use a neutral-coloured mount and leave the captioned edge of the photograph visible inside. Neutral colours for mounts work well with

modern photographs, although sometimes a contemporary black-and-white photograph can be set off by a more brightly coloured mount.

With an old portrait photograph, there is plenty of scope. Again, it would probably be unsuitable to crop it and give it a modern setting. A fabric mount, damask or lace perhaps, gives a period touch to a photograph. Alternatively, you could use old-fashioned marbled paper or vellum. In some cases, if the photograph is in good condition, it is possible to frame it directly, without using a mount. This may be especially effective in cases where older photographs have been 'vignetted' — that is, where the image is isolated in the centre of a slightly faded and misty-looking background.

One remarkable way to give a sympathetic setting to most old photographs is to use a fabric-covered frame. Leather can be glued onto a wooden frame, adding textural interest to the picture as a whole. Brown or olive green leather, for instance, works well with the warm tones of old

The collection of photographs (above, far left) is given cohesion by the formal arrangement and each one is made much more distinctive by the ruled lines that surround each photograph (see project, page 112). The sepia photograph (below, far left) is given a touch of colour by the fine strips of green and mid-brown inlay set in the wooden frame. The double mount beautifully sets off the modern print (left). By inserting strips of black into the light-coloured frame (above), the eye is drawn to the simple black-and-white print.

sepia photographs but any thick material can be used, including velvet and suede.

You can be much more boisterous in the treatment of modern photographs: black-and-white prints can be contrasted with brightly coloured surrounds; coloured photographs can be placed in a black-and-white setting or in a setting or colour which repeats a theme present in the photograph.

Modern photographs usually look their best in an austere setting, although this depends on the subject. A picture in the style of a contemporary photographer such as Ansell Adams, for instance, with its stark quality, sharply defined shapes and contrasting tones would be shown to best advantage in a simple frame — perhaps just a narrow metallic band or a plain black frame. Most modern photographs look best with as little distraction as possible and simple Perspex clipboards are usually sufficient, especially if the picture is to be hung against a plain background.

In modern photo-journalism the image is all-important and the subject is sometimes a serious one, often making a social comment or recording some dramatic event. Again, a fussy frame would be distracting and inappropriate.

PRINTS

There is a brisk market nowadays for prints of all kinds and ages, from faded illustrations torn from old books to bright, graphic lithographs produced by modern artists. As with photographs, contemporary prints can be freely interpreted when it comes to choosing a frame. Simple frames, such as those made of coloured plastic or metal strip, often look effective on strong modern designs.

There is one general rule which applies to both old and new prints: leave the edge of the print showing. In a good print, this edge should be a crisp line but all edges are interesting because they show how the plate is registered — that is, how the colours are laid on top of each other, so that they meet in the exact positions in the composition. With etch-

Posters

Because posters have such a strong graphic content, they nearly always require the simplest of frames. A blue mount and a flat blue frame surround the poster (above). In some cases, posters can look attractive without any surround at all—as with the poster (left), which has been clipped onto a backing board beneath glass. Transparent Perspex clips were used and the backing board was edged with plain wooden battens to give a neater edge (see project, page 100).

The traditional look
This piece of modern needlework was given a traditional appearance by surrounding it with a velvet-covered slip and a mahogany moulding.

Antique piece
This sampler requires an old-looking surround. It is well worth hunting for the right old-style frame for such an attractive piece.

ings, for instance, an indentation can be seen in the paper where the metal plate was pressed onto the damp paper. By leaving this 'key' intact when you frame the print, you display a facet of the production which many will find interesting.

Old prints can be given a new lease of life by reframing them. The white surround is often discoloured and frequently there will be blotches of mould, or foxing, which is caused by a chemical reaction of moisture in the atmosphere with the iron content in the paper. By reframing the print and giving it a mount, you can often cover up such defects. You will also have had an opportunity to clean up the print before reframing it. Cleaning, care and maintenance is covered in Care and Repair.

When reframing, you do not necessarily have to use an exact replica of the original frame but it is best if you choose one that remains in character with the picture. For example, a modern steel frame would look wrong with an antique print. Experiment with one of the finishes discussed on pages 44–47: the frame could be enhanced perhaps by a gilding or by a patina — a softening tonal wash.

Old prints often have the title underneath the picture. Rather than obliterating this, it is better to cut a small window in the mount.

POSTERS
The inspiration for most posters came from the events for which they were produced to advertise. Thus they began as ephemeral things, pieces of art which were by nature temporary. It is therefore often inappropriate to give them a permanent-looking frame, as if they were classical artefacts. Posters, after all, were designed to stand alone, and they can look striking if this effect is preserved. A simple block mount or clip frame is enough. For details of this style of mounting, see the poster project on pages 100–103.

Recently, posters have been more consciously aimed at being works of art in their own right and, there are many 'art' posters on the market. Yet they still reflect the original bold styles and, like prints, look best when framed in a simple way.

NEEDLEWORK AND OTHER FABRIC IMAGES
The way to prevent a piece of treasured needlework, collage, weaving or silk-screen from becoming tattered or worn is to frame it. The piece of work should be stretched first around a board or similar surface, fixing it at the back with masking tape. Until this is done, it is impossible to know its correct measurements for framing.

Glass is needed to protect the piece but avoid placing glass directly onto the surface. An insert or some other means must be found to separate the fabric from the glass pane where the material could be distorted by pressure from the glass.

In the late nineteenth and early twentieth centuries in America and Europe, embroidered samplers were often placed in tortoiseshelled, woodgrained or otherwise decorated frames and you

Maps and documents
The antique map of Africa (left) has been given a light wooden moulding with green edges. Because there is a lot of space within the actual subject, it does not need a separate mount. A red mount with a traditional tiny black and gilt frame adds a *theatrical formality to the small opera souvenir (below left). The simple black script on paper (below) is given a formal appearance by its plain red mount and polished wooden frame.*

might like to preserve this traditon when framing or reframing such a piece; finishes are discussed on pages 44–47.

MAPS AND DOCUMENTS — OLD AND NEW

It is best to separate quite clearly in your mind the difference between framing a modern map or document and an antique one. The two types are found on the wall for entirely different reasons: the antique one is there mainly for its visual effect, a decorative piece of nostalgia or historic interest; the modern one is there as a colourful reference.

Maps

For the modern map, a simple clip frame or block mount is preferable — a businesslike frame. Some might feel that the style of the frame will make no difference and that a modern map could be set within an old-looking elaborate frame but you will probably find that the result will look incongruous.

Genuinely antique maps, or reproductions of antiques that convey the same atmosphere, are often seen in frames of polished wood such as maple and walnut — woods with warm colours. They can also look good in frames decorated with a special finish, such as imitation tortoiseshell or marble *(see pages 93–97)*. Making a new frame for an old map provides an opportunity to carry out some finishing work to give the frame an antique look.

With an old map, the question immediately arises of whether to trim the edges to remove torn and grubby pieces of the paper edge. This is not advisable, especially if you have been lucky enough to get hold of a map which has not been interfered with too much over the years. Unfortunately, if the map is genuinely old, you are likely to find that it has

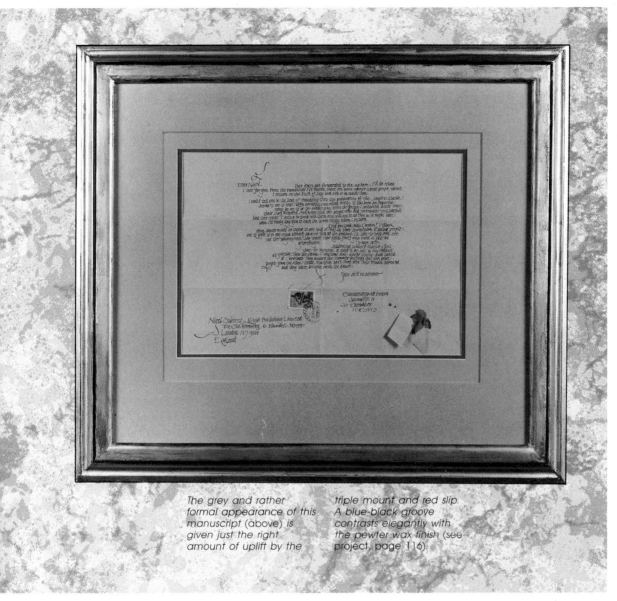

The grey and rather formal appearance of this manuscript (above) is given just the right amount of uplift by the triple mount and red slip. A blue-black groove contrasts elegantly with the pewter wax finish (see project, page 116).

already been trimmed too much, as different owners have forced it into available frames. Once removed, an edge cannot be replaced and the map will lose its value as well as the aesthetic effect of the original wide margin. Repair and cleaning of old maps and documents is explained on pages 136–137.

The broad margin which surrounds most old maps makes it generally undesirable to mount them. The margin itself, often with attractively aged and faded paper and interesting keys or titles, is a good enough 'mount' with which to surround the map.

With an old map, or any piece of archive document that you wish to preserve and frame, it is advisable to flatten out the original carefully and place it on a conservation board; the board should be specially purchased. Ordinary mounting board will not do in this case as it absorbs the acid in the air,

and this will eventually soak through into the print and discolour or damage it.

Some interesting maps and documents, which you might wish to frame, are printed on both sides. In order that you can see both sides, a double-sided frame, usually a freestanding one, is necessary. Double-sided frames are often used when framing bonds and shares.

Documents

These also fit into two basic categories: the functional, such as a diploma, which is there to inform; and the decorative, such as a piece of calligraphy, an historic manuscript or an illuminated text. With the functional document, a simple frame is better: a plain narrow frame reflects its dignity. With the decorative piece, the choice is broader. A piece of writing is essentially flat, without the illusion of space

Pressed flowers
The attraction of these pressed flowers (above) lies partly in their fragile and faded look. The collector browsed through the junk shops to find this fitting old, plain, narrow frame.

found in most pictures and, for this reason, it is often rewarding to give a spatial feeling to a piece of text by placing it in a frame with moulding that projects outwards to make the whole object three-dimensional. Illuminated lettering is often decorated with gold and bright colours. This can be pleasingly brought out by having gilt on the frame and perhaps adding a narrow strip of one of the colours contained in the text.

THE THREE-DIMENSIONAL

Many people like to display a three-dimensional set piece on the wall. This might be a collection of medals, or a collage made of shells, beads or other materials. Oriental fans, tiny pieces of carvings or sculpture, or arrangements of dried flowers can all look attractive on a wall.

This type of piece calls for a box-like frame, sometimes known as a display frame or 'shadow box', so-called because when lit from an angle it can highlight the three-dimensional aspect of the piece

with shadows. The box is basically an ordinary frame but with a deeper insert.

Any subject which is likely to gather dust, such as dried flowers or a delicate fan, should be placed under glass. With the three-dimensional box, you can choose your own background to match the subject. If it is a Chinese fan, for instance, a piece of Chinese paper would make a good background; shells could be placed on a 'beach' effect made by glueing sand evenly across the back board. There is plenty of scope here for creativity.

Extra care is needed for work of a more enduring nature, such as ceramics, jewellery and small pieces of sculpture or antique glass. Such items stand out alone, and often need the simplest of settings. A piece of Roman glass, for instance, is intrinsically interesting and invites close inspection. Such a hard and glossy object would benefit from being placed on a simple, softly textured background which complements the centrepiece, such as coarse silk or linen.

Shadow boxes
For the butterflies (above), a deep moulding was chosen to create a space between the glass and the fragile subjects. Like the butterflies, the jewels (right) were also mounted on black velvet to accentuate them. The glass front of the jewellery frame forms a lid, which gives access to the contents.

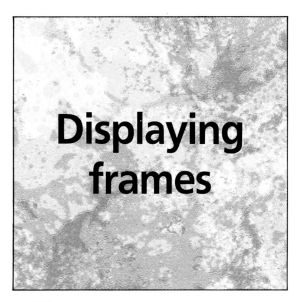

Displaying frames

There is a view — some might call it artistic snobbery — that it is wrong to consider how a painting will fit in with the decor of a room. Painting, they argue, is on a high aesthetic plane far superior to such mundane things as interior decorating. However, this argument ignores the fact that throughout its early history most art was created purely to complement its surroundings.

While the more experimental art forms play an undeniably important cultural role, it would be a pity if the pleasure of choosing pictures and frames to suit the home environment was lost and this section looks at the place of the frame within the larger environment of a room.

PLACING THE ARTPIECE

When deciding where to hang a framed artpiece, several practical points should be borne in mind. Heat can seriously damage the surface of paintings, especially oils, so avoid placing them directly above heaters. Not only will the rising heat damage the picture but dust and grease will also be carried upwards and will gradually concentrate over the picture surface. If for some reason you cannot avoid placing a picture above a heater, then make sure that it is glazed. Artworks should also be kept free of damp and condensation. Direct sunlight can cause watercolours to fade; some pigments are especially vulnerable. A popular material used in modern watercolours is watercolour concentrate, such as Lumar; some of these colours are particularly fugitive. Hang such paintings on walls that are not in the line of direct sunlight.

Aesthetic considerations are also important. If you have only one artpiece on a wall it is usually preferable to hang it so that the centre of the artpiece aligns approximately with the average person's eye-level. This position will vary according to the room in which the artpiece is hung: if you wish to hang a set of pictures in a hallway, for instance,

where people rarely sit, then eye-level should be determined when standing; in a sitting-room, however, you should hang the pictures lower as people are likely to view them from a chair or sofa.

A small or narrow space — a hallway or corridor, for instance — is often ideal for small, detailed artpieces, where the interest lies in the content rather than in the general visual impact. A larger picture, however, where the viewer needs to stand back in order to take in the whole image, requires more space. It may look impressive at the end of a long corridor, or you could try placing it opposite the entrance to a room.

GROUPING AND ARRANGING

Often, the striking characteristic of a group of artpieces is their unity: they all seem to belong. This effect does not happen automatically; much thought is needed to achieve it. Attention should be given to the space between each artpiece. If the space is too narrow, the pictures will interfere with each other, whereas if there is too much space, the group will lose its cohesion.

Before hanging a group of pictures, it is a good idea to arrange them on the floor first, matching the shapes and colours. This will give you a reasonable

Vertical arrangement
The arrangement of the frames here (above) have an effect on the appearance of the interior of the hallways as a whole. The irregular rectangles form a pillar of their own and complement the diagonal slope of the banisters and the curved arch of the open doorway.

Colourful abundance
Frames need not be regularly spaced in a formal way. They can often look attractive when thrown together at random, completely covering a wall to present an effect rather like an antique market or junk shop. In the arrangement (right), a colourful mixture of antique and modern frames containing a variety of images creates an exciting impact.

The more formal approach
1 A few smaller frames can be ranged around a very large picture to good effect. Align the tops to give a formal cohesion to the group.
2 Four rectangular frames, each of a different size and proportion, can be given form by basing them on vertical and horizontal axes.
3 Arrange a variety of rectangular frames sitting on top and hanging underneath a hypothetical line
4 This mixture of frames are arranged within what is in effect an overall 'frame'—the rectangle in which they are enclosed.
5 When arranging frames on the wall of a stairway, use imaginary verticals to provide form. In this way a 'scattered', unrelated look is avoided.

1

2

3

4

5

Arranging and displaying

Period frames are arranged symmetrically and aligned with a sideboard to give a neat effect (top left). Circular objects provide an interesting contrast (centre top). A set of framed pictures (top right) gives a formal appearance to this elegant bedroom. A set of cards is given form by the fan-shaped frame (far left). As the frame is transparent, its shape does not disrupt the wall colour. A bathroom is enlivened with framed documents and charts (left). A dense arrangement of pictures makes a feature of a whole wall (right).

representation of the final effect and the opportunity to experiment before you commit yourself.

One way of making a harmonious group from an array of different shapes and odd proportions is to line up either the tops or the bottoms of the pictures. If you are arranging a group of artpieces for an awkward space, such as the wall next to a staircase, it is not always practical to align them horizontally. In this case, the group spirit can be preserved by lining up the sides of the pictures so that there are regular 'columns' of space between them. Other groupings that can work well include square and circular formations. Experiment with different arrangements to see which suits your artworks best.

MIXING AND MATCHING FRAMES

A set of matching artpieces, or even very different ones, can be given unity by placing each one in an identical frame. This is especially effective if there are other things in the room which are visually 'busy', such as patterned fabrics and wallpapers.

However, one of the most exciting forms of design for a group is to mix the frames, mixing not only the colours, shapes, styles and sizes but also old and new. Although a room that is decorated in a particular period style requires frames that do not jar with the style, most rooms are not designed in such a unified way. Rooms are more often designed according to personal taste and, over a period of years, result in a mixture, which can often benefit from a grouping of pictures and frames that mingles old and new styles and materials. Place a modern plastic frame beside an older-looking wooden moulding, and they may set each other off attractively. Sometimes an oval frame sits nicely in a group of rectangular ones, giving just the right amount of variation. Try to preserve some visual unity, however, or the result will appear random and chaotic.

When it comes to mounts, the scope is unlimited. You can design your mounts to fit into a particular room, or to suit a particular group of images. As mounts čan be changed without harming the pictures, there is plenty of room for experiment.

LIGHTING

If you decide to light your artpiece, you are faced with two alternatives. You can either 'spot' it, by placing an ordinary light or spotlight to shine on it from elsewhere in the room, or you can fix lighting on or near the frame itself.

Traditionally, painters have used natural light, often a skylight or northern light, to work by and many painters still follow this tradition. Ideally, therefore, pictures should be lit by daylight from above or from a northerly direction — in other words, 'soft' daylight — but this is rarely practical. Electric bulbs are available which imitate daylight and some galleries use fluorescent lighting under a casing of pearly plastic; long strips of lights are sometimes set in brackets, either above or below the picture. Such lighting techniques could be used in a large room to highlight oil paintings but are not advisable with glazed pictures, as the glass tends to reflect the light detracting from the picture.

Most of us prefer to use normal domestic lighting so that the artpiece blends in with the rest of the room, although, for a special picture, you could make some adjustments. It might be worth buying lighting strips to fit into brackets and attach to the frame itself to look downwards or upwards at the picture, or you may achieve an attractive effect by fixing a spotlight to the ceiling or wall and directing the light at the picture. If you dislike the harshness of spotlights, position ordinary household lighting, such as standard lamps or table lamps, in such a way that they provide good lighting for the pictures. Specially placed lights and spots can be hidden behind a piece of furniture or among plants. Experiment until you achieve exactly the effect that you want.

Variety of style
The use of different shapes, sizes and types of frame bring this bedroom to life (right). Because the arrangement is interesting, the eye is led to each picture. By mixing bold frames with unstriking frames that blend with the colour scheme of the room, the overall appearance is never overwhelming.

Lighting and wiring

For more complex arrangements of framed pictures, lighting becomes important. Care must be taken not to beam a light onto a frame in such a way that a deep moulding creates a shadow across part of the picture. Wiring should also be kept as invisible as possible. These pictures and free-standing figures (right) have been lit in such a way that wiring is not too obtrusive. The movable spotlights in the ceiling can be adjusted to emphasize different artworks or aspects of a collection.

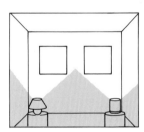
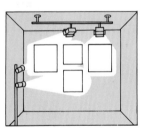
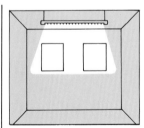
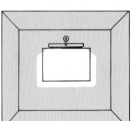

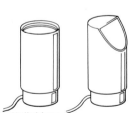

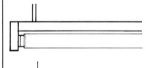

Uplighters
Pictures can be lit by directing lamps from beneath. Special uplighting units create an even, diffused light, spreading upwards and outwards. These are sometimes grouped together to produce an area of even light across the top part of a room or gallery.

Spots
Spotlights can be adjusted to create direct or reflected light. These can run on a strip track, attached to or hung below the ceiling. Single spots can be fixed to the wall, ceiling or floor, and can also be bought fixed to a stand. Use them singly or in groups.

Strips
Sometimes an arrangement of framed pictures looks best when lit by one source. For this, a strip of fluorescent lighting is ideal. Light can be directed onto the pictures by deflectors.

Picture lamps
Individual picture lamps can be bought in a variety of sizes and shapes to suit almost every type of picture. A range of styles is available, from antiqued and old-fashioned to modern designs.

Mounts and mounting

I t is important to differentiate clearly between the mount — the 'window' which is placed upon the artwork — and the backing card or board onto which the artwork is stuck before the process begins. Confusion arises because this backing is often referred to as the mount. The means by which the artwork is stuck to this backing is also referred to as 'mounting'. This section discusses the general principles of mounts and mounting. The specific techniques are dealt with in clear, detailed, step-by-step terms in the section entitled the Foundation Skills.

THE BREATHING SPACE

Many artpieces are mounted as well as framed. In other words, the picture does not make direct contact with the frame but is surrounded by a wide margin which separates the picture from the frame. This is the mount. It is the 'breathing space' between the picture content and the frame itself.

There are no rigid rules governing whether you should or should not have a mount within your frame but, as a basic guideline, consider the artpiece itself: does it, for instance, contain large areas of empty space in its composition, as in the case of a line drawing on a plain white background? This sort of picture would look effective with only a small amount of border, or possibly with none at all. On the other hand, a more crowded picture would benefit from a substantial border of space between the image and the frame.

The mount should be chosen before the frame, because it is the mount that comes next to the artpiece. A great deal of mystery has been attached to the 'proportions' of the mount — the amount of space which should be left at the bottom, sides and top of the image. In fact, the choice is personal and there is nothing magical about the measurements. There are some general rules, however.

The proportions of the mount should not compete with the proportions of the artwork; that is, a big picture does not necessarily need a wide mount and a small picture does not always benefit from having a narrow mount. Generally speaking, a small picture is much improved by a wide mount and a grand-looking frame. Do not follow this principle slavishly or you will end up with a postage-stamp-size picture in the middle of a poster-size mount! There are some exceptions. Small photographs can sometimes look good with narrow mounts. A flamboyant modern print can benefit from a wide mount. The result is usually more effective if you avoid giving the visual impression that you have used exactly the same area for the mount as for the artpiece.

There is one important visual illusion which needs

Mount widths
The width of the mount has an immediate effect on the framed picture as a whole. If the mount is too small, it can give the picture a cramped and restricted look. An equal all-round width works well with some images. If the mount is large in comparison with the picture, it is usually better if the picture 'sits' high up in the frame—make sure the mount margin at the bottom of the picture is deeper than that of the other three sides.

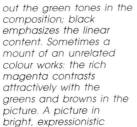

Choosing a colour
The landscape (top) is painted in muted, earthy colours. With a picture like this, it is usually advisable to choose a colour that harmonizes with the subject. The light beige mount makes the picture look darker; the dull olive green immediately picks

out the green tones in the composition; black emphasizes the linear content. Sometimes a mount of an unrelated colour works: the rich magenta contrasts attractively with the greens and browns in the picture. A picture in bright, expressionistic

colours (above) poses a very different problem. The mount generally should be as strong and bright as the colours contained in the painting. The red, blue, yellow, pink and mauve mounts all emphasize these particular colours in the portrait. The lime green

provides a contrast; the white mount is effective because it picks out the background of the picture, giving a light, spacious feel.

31

Assembling block frames
For a neat finish, block frames can be edged with wooden battens and clips screwed into these. The framer (right) is using Perspex clips, which do not intrude upon the image. These clips are also available in brass and stainless steel.

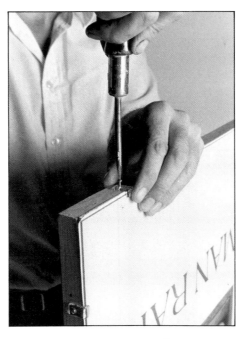

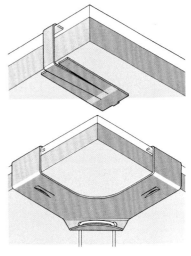

Alternative clips
Spring clips (top) and metal corner pieces (above) are found in most framers' supply shops.

to be considered. If the width of space around an artpiece is equal, then the bottom will appear smaller than the other margins. Therefore, an impression of symmetry is best produced by having the space at the bottom a little larger than the other margins — between 6mm (¹/₄in) and 18mm (³/₄in) is enough in most cases, depending on the size of the artpiece.

THE BASIC MOUNT
Mounting card is available in three different thicknesses: 4-sheet (1000 microns), 6-sheet (1250 microns) and 8-sheet (1900 microns). 6-sheet is the most commonly used and available in the widest variety of colours: maroon, saxe blue, green, grey, pompadour, pale green, holly green, Russian green, mid grey, bottle green, sepia, seal, coffee, ivory and poster black. 8-sheet is the thickest of the three. Thicker card is available but is quite often difficult to obtain and you will probably have to resort to sticking thin pieces of card together if you want to achieve a thick mount. A thick mount is necessary if you wish to create a deeper recess for your picture. For example, if you are working with a very small image and you want to exaggerate its smallness, fragility or preciousness, you might want a deeply recessed effect.

Block Mounts
With modern photographs, a popular method is to use a 'block' mount, in which the image juts out to meet the viewer instead of receding inside a 'window' as is usually the case. Block mounting is inexpensive and simple to do. The photograph can be trimmed first to remove any white edge. Then it is fixed onto a platform, or block, usually of chipboard or wood, which can be hung as it is or stuck onto a flat surface to leave a surround.

CO-ORDINATING THE COLOURS
As with space, the colours of mount and artpiece should not compete with or equal each other. The colour of the mount should not overpower or merge with the colours in the picture. On the whole, the colours of the mount should not be too strong or bright but should be muted and neutral.

Sometimes, contrast can be effective: warm colours in a picture can be offset by a cool colour in the mount, and vice versa. For instance, a sepia drawing can be enhanced by a grey, pale blue or pale green surround. Traditionally, watercolours are given cool-coloured mounts, perhaps because of their mainly delicate washes and subjects, although in recent years dark green and brown have become popular, especially for landscapes. The darker the mount, the more quickly the eye is drawn towards the picture.

With many modern prints, the rules of co-ordination are discarded in favour of dramatic effect and instant impact. Bright colours can often successfully surround a modern print to produce a startling and eye-catching effect.

Mounts are usually made from mounting card. This is available in a variety of colours but, if you are seeking an unusual colour or a different pattern or texture, it is quite possible to buy plain white card and stick coloured or hand-decorated paper onto it.

If you are using acid-free conservation board — for instance, for an old map or document — you may find that this is available in only white or off-white. Again, you can stick a good quality paper — that is, a hand-made paper produced from rags, which is relatively free from impurities — onto an acid-free board. Do not use the usual spray adhesive or commercial glues in this case; you must buy acid-free tape from an art shop or make your own paste from wheatflour and water, otherwise the chemical glue fumes may damage the picture.

WINDOWS

On deciding to use a mount, you are not limited to a single rectangle for the window. You can, if you wish, 'trim' your picture — without actually cutting it — by placing a differently shaped window on top of it. Or you can simply use a window which suits the shape of the original picture.

One extremely effective way in which to set certain artworks, but a more difficult one to cut, is an oval or round mount. Ovals are particularly attractive for mounting vignettes; small pictures which do not have hard edges. Oval and circular-shaped mounts are available from art shops in standard sizes ready-cut.

If you require a specific size which is not available ready-cut, and you do not have access to an oval mount cutter, then it is best to hand-cut ovals and circles, using a scalpel or art knife — and great care. You may need considerable practice with scraps of card before you are ready to cut the final piece but other devices are available, such as compass-cutters and templates.

For the adventurous and the skilled, it is possible to cut an endless variety of window shapes. You do not have to follow any particular traditions, although bizarre shapes can look rather ridiculous unless they are particularly suited to the picture and are well designed. It is advisable to use thin card rather than mounting board, at least until you become more skilled and confident.

An artwork can be made to look richer and more expensive by setting it in a double mount, cutting an inner mount which fits under the main one, so that only a small part of the inner mount shows. This small band can be more adventurous than the main mount, perhaps using a bright colour or even gilt. A third mount can be added, although care is needed in the choice of colour and size — too many confusing edges tend to detract from the artwork.

If you have a collection or series of small artpieces that go well together, they can be set within the same frame. This is called a multiple mount. Two, three, four, six or eight pictures can best be mounted together. This obviously takes a little planning and the layout requires thought. It is advisable to set out the pictures on a piece of paper and then to cut windows from the paper. Use this paper pattern as a guide for the final mount.

THE BEVELLED EDGE

Almost all mounts are cut with a bevelled edge. Instead of cutting a piece of board or card with the knife held vertically, the cutting edge is sloped. Thus, instead of a sheer 'canyon' effect, the picture is placed in a window which has inclining sides. This means that no unwanted trace of shadow will appear, and the eye will be brought directly to the picture without hindrance from a hard edge.

Ready-made mounts
Ready-made mounts (below) are available in a variety of shapes, sizes and colours. Buy mounts made from rag fibres — those containing wood pulp can cause staining.

Multi-window mounts
An attractive display can be created by using multi-window mounts (right). There is no set number of windows that should be cut in a single card, but spacing is crucial and you should try various arrangements before cutting. Pictures that relate to each other can often be visually linked in this way.

Bevelled edges
Cutting a bevelled edge requires practice, and it is best to experiment first on scraps of card. Keep the knife at a constant angle when cutting. It is essential to have a really sharp scalpel or knife.

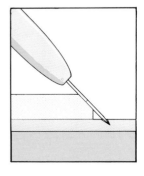

Bought mounts
Mounts can be bought in a rich variety of finishes. In this collection, pale, thin washes contrast with ribboned and marbled borders.
1 *Blue and gold French wash mount.*
2 *Peach and gold English wash-line mount.*
3,5,7 *Line, gold line and wash mounts.*
4,6,8 *Marbled mounts with*

contrasting overmounts.
9,10 *Marbled mounts with coloured undermounts.*
11 *Blue-grey marbled mount.*
12 *Taupe marbled mount.*
13 *Cream marbled mount.*
14 *Gold line and wash.*
15 *Green wash.*
16 *Reverse-bevel double mount.*
17 *Marbled mount.*
18 *Yellow wash mount.*
19 *Grey wash mount.*

20 *Pink wash mount.*
21 *Blue wash mount.*
22 *Pink wash mount.*
23 *Line-and-wash mount.*
24 *Marbled mount with contrasting overmount.*
25 *Mulberry paper mount with ribbon inlay.*
26 *Line-and-wash mount.*
27 *Marbled mount with contrasting overmount.*
28 *Line-and-wash, two-tone mount with inlay.*

Bevelling evenly by hand is quite difficult. Again, practice is the answer and an extremely sharp cutting tool is vital. Use a metal ruler fixed in position to guide your hand when cutting such an edge. It is possible to obtain a mount cutter, a tool which holds replaceable blades in position, (see page 54) but this tool is difficult to get used to and it can take just as long to learn how to use it as to become proficient in cutting by hand.

A fine finishing touch can be given to a bevelled edge by gilding it or painting it in a contrasting colour.

LINES AND WASHES

There is a refinement which can be added to the process of mounting to give the finished product a genuinely period touch. Lines and washes became popular in Europe during the eighteenth century and the technique is known as French mounting — an arrangement of lines, sometimes filled with a light wash, set around the picture. The point of the arrangement is to guide the eye gently in to the painting or drawing.

Colours are crucial to this process. They must be chosen carefully to complement those in the picture itself. A common mistake is to make them too brash. The secret is to 'understate' rather than 'overstate'. Otherwise, you will find that when you view the finished product, you notice the lines instead of the picture, which defeats the whole purpose.

Lines and washes work best on a neutral-coloured mount, one which does not challenge the arrangement. If you have only a dark-coloured or soiled mount, cover it with watercolour paper before applying lines and washes. The lines themselves are often drawn in gold, producing the luxurious effect which has been traditionally popular. Many people will have frequently looked at watercolours surrounded by lines and washes, without noticing that the technique has been used. This is because it has been done with subtlety.

The use of lines and washes became common in Europe towards the end of the eighteenth century and was still popular in the nineteenth. This was when the classical school of English watercolourists came into its own, reaching great heights with such artists as John Sell Cotman (1782–1842) and Thomas Girtin (1775–1802). The lines and washes employed on the mounts for their pictures have become so familiar, and are so subtly done that we scarely notice them.

Framers still rely on the line-and-wash method when they want to give an extra finish to the product. The method, although traditionally used with neutral colours by the watercolourists, is nowadays sometimes used on vibrant, modern prints. In this case the line and wash is often bolder, using brighter colours for both the wash and the lines.

One of the attractive features of the line-and-wash technique is that you are not limited. You can vary the width of line, the space between the lines

Line-and-wash borders
An English Lady by Hans Holbein (above) has a line-and-wash border, which is painted onto the picture itself. Modern lines and washes include: **1** silver, white, gold and red on light grey; **2** silver and light grey on Wedgewood blue; **3** black, gold and white on cream; **4** Ochre edged with gold, with a fine black line.

Fabric coverings
Mounts and frames can be covered by an enormous variety of materials. Velvet, leather, silk, hessian — there is a host of different textures and patterns to choose from. They can be used to cover the outer frames or mounts, which will add a dash of colour to the artpiece. Spend time experimenting with fabrics, placing them beside pictures to see how they work. Learn how to enhance a picture without overwhelming it. For a less dominant tonal or textural effect, fabrics can also be used for just part of a frame or mount, limited, for instance, to the borders.

and the number of lines. You also have a choice of colour. You can use only one colour, or you can be adventurous and use several.

Do not launch into the technique without careful preparation. You will need to practise first: try using a mount wash kit (available from art shops) to begin with if you are unused to painting with watercolours. Traditionally, an ordinary nibbed pen was used and craftsmen developed great skill in keeping the lines even and in varying their width, by making confident movements with the pen and ensuring that it did not run out of ink at a crucial time, producing an uneven or broken rule.

Today, we are much luckier. Ruling pens are easily available from art and graphic suppliers; these have adjustable nibs, so that the same pen can be used whatever sort of line you are making. The pen is specially made so that the nib effectively acts as a tiny reservoir to ensure a smooth flow of ink.

COVERING A MOUNT

Mounts can be covered with a variety of materials, not only to produce different colours but to give a variety of textural effects. Two of the most popular materials are hessian and linen, easily obtainable from fabric shops. Mounting card can be bought already covered with canvas, hessian or silk but in this case the bevelled edge remains uncovered. Fabric of this kind is also often used to cover the wooden insert of a frame for oil or acrylic paintings to give a suitably textured area between the frame

and the painted surface.

A fabric mount can also be used to put a picture in context. For example, an early twentieth-century silhouette or an old portrait photograph could be given a period flavour by using taffeta or shot silk on the mount. Black or deep red velvet could be effective in giving a luxurious feel to a grand picture or to lend distinction and formality to a collection of medals or coins, and a suede or leather mount makes a treasured photograph more enduring and special. Many modern pictures are enhanced by a mount covered in a soft textural weave, such as hessian, canvas or linen. Artists' canvas comes in a range of subtle tones from off-white to a muted dark beige.

Paper, too, has its different textures. Shiny and metallic surfaces can be used as surrounds. In some cases, why not use textured wallpaper? Many people underestimate the amazing variety of patterns available nowadays in paper. Particularly interesting are the unusual, though sometimes expensive, papers used in the bookbinding craft. These include many beautiful marbled patterns and some intricate designs, subtle enough to be useful to the picture framer.

WET AND DRY MOUNTING

As well as deciding on the mount, you must ensure that the artwork itself is stuck firmly onto a backing. Frequently, the works that you wish to frame will not have been executed directly onto paper thick or

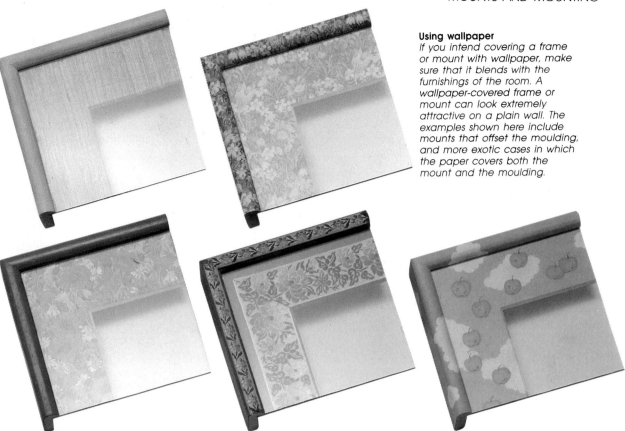

Using wallpaper
If you intend covering a frame or mount with wallpaper, make sure that it blends with the furnishings of the room. A wallpaper-covered frame or mount can look extremely attractive on a plain wall. The examples shown here include mounts that offset the moulding, and more exotic cases in which the paper covers both the mount and the moulding.

firm enough to support them without this backing material being added before the artwork is taped to the backing board. Remember that if you are dealing with valuable, old or treasured pictures or documents, acid-free conservation board should be used.

The methods used by craftsmen for sticking the picture to a stiff card or board are known as 'wet mounting' and 'dry mounting'.

Wet mounting simply means glueing a picture onto a board, but this has to be done with great care — it is all too easy to end up with bubbles or ridges, and a treasured picture can be ruined.

First a piece of board or card is cut to exactly the same size as the artwork itself. Then an adhesive, preferably a rubber- or plastic-based glue, is brushed smoothly or sprayed evenly on top and the picture carefully positioned. To smooth out the bubbles and any excess glue, it is flattened with a roller or cloth, moving towards the edges from the centre. It is advisable to clamp the picture and backing between boards while the glue is drying.

A more permanent professional finish is achieved by dry mounting. A sheet of adhesive wax film (available from art and craft shops) is carefully placed between the picture and its backing and the film is then heated to fuse the picture or print to the backing card, giving a perfect product. Professionals use dry-mounting presses but these are expensive. Dry mounting can be done just as effectively by using a regular household iron.

TAPING

If the picture is stiff enough without a backing, or if you do not want to take the irretrievable step of fusing the artpiece to the backing, use tape. Strips of fabric or masking tape should be used, rather than normal transparent tape, as they can be unstuck comparatively easily.

Very narrow tape is usually sufficient for this process. It can be positioned so that it overlaps both the edge of the picture and the backing card, or — if you do not want to stick it onto the top surface of the picture or print — you can fold the tape back onto itself as you would with stamps in an album, creating a double-sided adhesive tape effect. Double-sided tape is not a wise alternative: as with clear tape, it is too firmly adhesive and can cause difficulties should you wish to remove the artwork at a later date. It is also more difficult to position the artwork correctly using double-sided tape.

HINGE MOUNTS

One way of ensuring that you position an artpiece, exactly in place on a backing is to construct a hinge mount. Simply hinge the backing onto the window and close them together, placing the artwork in between the two *(see pages 58–61 for details)*. One advantage of this method is that the window mount and backing are fixed permanently in relation to each other, allowing you to move the picture around on the inner backing until you have found exactly the right position for it.

THE PRINCIPLES OF FRAMING

Types of moulding

The mould is the frame itself, the outer edges that most people have in mind when they think of a frame. Moulding is available in the form of strips of wood similar to the carved pieces that surround many doors and windows. This section discusses the types of moulding available for making your own frames, and the variety of finishes you can apply to them. Specific details on the techniques of measuring, cutting, glueing and finishing frames are given in clear, step-by-step format in the section called Foundation Skills.

There are two types of moulding: framers' moulding and builders' moulding. The main difference between the two is that framers' moulding comes with a fitted rebate; that is, it is 'stepped' in order to allow the picture, mount and glass to fit neatly into place without falling right through the frame.

Builders' moulding is primarily intended for trimming doors, windows, skirting boards and for other interior finishes. Its use as picture-framing material is incidental and, consequently, it does not have a fitted rebate. Consequently, if you use builders' moulding, you will either have to cut out the step or create a recess by sticking a narrow strip of wood underneath the moulding.

The other important difference is the price. Framers' moulding is very expensive. It comes prefinished and is often made of hardwood. However, for the amateur, it is advisable to use framers' moulding initially despite the extra cost because the added complication of having to make rebates is something that can well be left until you have more frame-making experience.

Once you have a little experience, you may want to use builders' moulding. At this stage, when you visit a builders' yard or timber shop, you will probably be surprised at the wide variety of mouldings available Many can be used as picture frames and sometimes two or more types can be put together to make a more elaborate frame.

When browsing through the yards and shops for builders' framing, bear in mind the width of the framing you will need — the picture should not be overshadowed. For a classical or traditional oil painting, a heavy moulding several inches wide is desirable; for a more abstract design, a simpler edging is preferable.

One advantage of using builders' moulding is that it gives a free range to home experts who wish to create their own finishes.

FRAMERS' MOULDING

Ready-made framers' moulding is available in a variety of types and finishes and is to be found in art shops and picture-framing stockists. There is an impressive array of mouldings from reproduction, antique-looking and highly decorated edgings to plain and simple styles.

Framers' mouldings include, at the exotic end of the range, the period mouldings, gilded and ornate, with delicate leaf-like patterns and elegant and formal ribbed designs reminiscent of the flamboyant courts of the *Ancien Régime* in eighteenth-century France. Also to be found are the more mundane, but attractive, spoon or scoop shapes in which the edging appears as if it has been scooped out regularly right along its line. Related to these are the traditional 'window frame' styles which 'step down' in gentle progression towards the picture.

Reproduction frames
From the simple to the extremely ornate, this selection gives an indication of the enormous range of reproduction framers' mouldings available today. They are known as:
1 *'Marlborough';* 2 *Red and gold;* 3 *'Van Huysum';* 4 *Red crackle;* 5 *Reproduction seventeenth-century;* 6 *'Rondo';* 7 *'Ripple';* 8 *Gilt Art Nouveau;* 9 *Black and gold;* 10 *Reproduction sixteenth-century Florentine;* 11 *Gilt;* 12 *'Whistler';* 13 *'Edgar Enigma';* 14 *Faux tortoiseshell;* 15 *'Aschkar';* 16 *'Old Ornate Bourlet';* 17 *'Klanaris';* 18 *Golf leaf on blue, no 11;* 19 *'Rembrandt';* 20 *Dutch veneer, no 6;* 21 *'Marco 1';* 22 *Gilt;* 23 *Red, black and gold;* 24 *Crackled green and bronze;* 25 *Gold leaf;* 26 *'Jap 1';* 27 *'Chinzan';* 28 *Hogarth;* 29 *Gilt;* 30 *Black Flemish-style.*

Variety of mouldings

Builders' moulding comes in a surprising amount of different styles. Become more familiar with the range by browsing in timber yards and do-it-yourself shops. Most timber shops have charts giving a 'to scale' range. You will need to make your own rebate.

Window board

Panel moulding

Skirting

Dado

Rebate half round

Architrave

Full round

Half round

Quadrant

Doorstop

Less expensive are the simple wood slopes and flat edges with aluminium finishes.

If you want a metal frame, it can usually be purchased in the form of straight metal strips. However, metal is more difficult to use than wood and special equipment is needed to drill and saw it *(see page 75)*. It is possible to obtain framers' moulding which is covered in a thin veneer of metal. This looks like solid metal but can be sawn and treated like any other moulding.

One of the more striking characteristics of the range of framers' mouldings available is the large variation in width. Here, keen judgement is necessary. Try to keep in mind the artpiece you are framing when looking over the strip of moulding.

Insert mouldings are also available from picture-frame stockists. They can be fitted inside the outer frame to give endless combinations of colour, shape and texture.

Much variation is provided, too, by different types of wood, each with its own characteristic appearance. One favourite is walnut but you will also find such woods as maple and cherry prominent on the shelves. Further alternatives include mouldings that have been stained, gilded, coloured or waxed.

BUILDERS' MOULDING

At first glance there seems to be less variety of builders' moulding than framers' moulding but great scope is available in the way builders' moulding can be combined and finished.

This is not so unusual as it may appear, for, if you look closely at the framers' mouldings available, you will often find that they themselves comprise subtle combinations of differently shaped strips.

One common type of builders' moulding found in the timber yards and do-it-yourself shops is the heavy, traditional carved strip often found around door frames. This automatically suggests itself for a picture in the grander style, such as a substantial oil painting; but with care and good finishing, some surprising effects are achieved by using this heavy style as a surround for a smaller image, such as a portrait. This can produce the effect of a dramatic

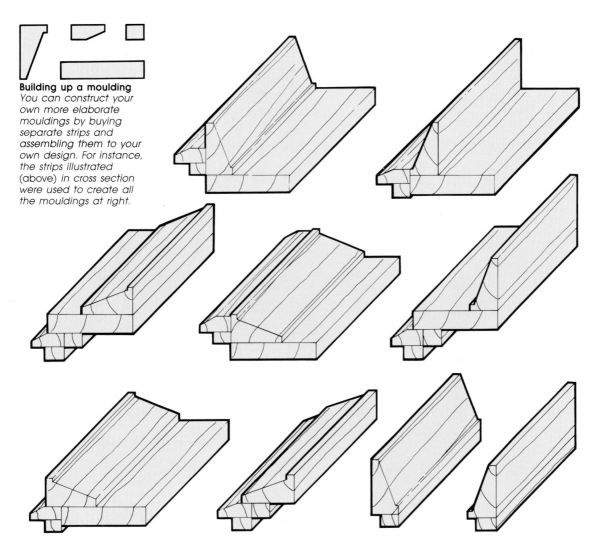

Building up a moulding
You can construct your own more elaborate mouldings by buying separate strips and assembling them to your own design. For instance, the strips illustrated (above) in cross section were used to create all the mouldings at right.

Moulding can often be attractively carved. Use existing frames for inspiration and keep the designs simple and tools very sharp.

recess, almost as if you are looking at the picture down a tunnel.

The door mouldings and the slightly smaller window strips are the obvious choices; they already look like most framers' mouldings. However, there are more unusual styles, such as symmetrical mouldings, where the inside edge is the same as the outside one, and rounded or bevelled beadings.

With builders' mouldings, if the exact profile you had in mind is not manufactured, then you can often come very close to it by combining two or more simpler pieces. If you can persuade your timber merchants' to give you waste pieces or offcuts with which to experiment in different combinations, you will soon become quite expert.

We should stress again the major difference between framers' and builders' mouldings — framers' strips come with a fitted rebate, builders' mouldings do not. Whichever moulding you choose, you must bear in mind the need for a rebate. If the basic moulding is wide enough you could, perhaps, make a rebate by gouging it out of the same piece

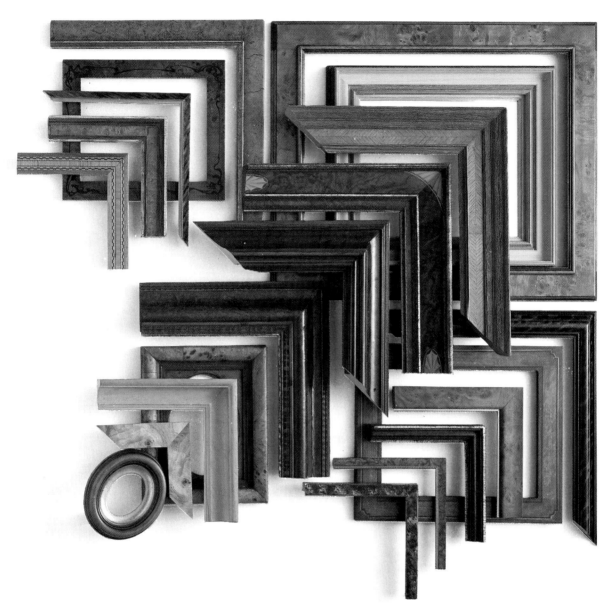

but this is complicated and can lead to mistakes. By far the simplest method is to stick a plain strip of wood to the back of the selected moulding*(see page 78).*

SELECTING THE FRAME

By using an appropriate style of frame you can set off your picture to advantage. When choosing a frame, bear in mind the period and style of the picture. A delicate Japanese print, for example, would not be complemented by a heavy European frame with an eighteenth-century look. Such a mismatch of styles would immediately jolt the senses.

However, selecting a frame is still more a question of personal taste than rules. For instance, many Impressionist and Post-impressionist paintings, their colours brighter and brushwork bolder than that of their predecessors, still look well inside the ornate

Bought frames and mouldings
A fine, grained frame with a raised inner edge stands complete at the top right of this selection. The group of grained woods and veneers illustrates the range of frames and mouldings available. At the bottom left-hand corner are two types of frame for an oval picture, including a gold slip oval that would enhance a particularly treasured period miniature. A more formal style of room cries out for the more formal, polished frames that are typical of those grouped together

here. Among the narrower frames is an elegant tortoiseshell and gold, two sides of which are illustrated at the top left. Next to it is a corner piece in antique walnut veneer. Some solid and grand frames lie across the centre of the group, including one with fan-shaped wooden inlays. Take care when choosing frames of this sort— consideration should be given not only to the type of picture to be framed, but also to the suitability of the frame to the environment where the picture will hang.

Colourful paint finishes
Some highly decorative paint finishes are featured in this group of mouldings. All ready-cut frames, they combine a traditional period flavour with modern experimental finishes. The yellow marbled frame across the centre is frankly faked. Yet the result is a tasteful version of a traditional marbling technique, even though the colours are chosen to blend well with a modern interior. It contrasts strongly with the simple green and turquoise ovals that lie next to it in the group. To their bottom right is a
series of specimens including a 'faux' or 'made' (imitation) malachite, and two elegant and narrow samples finished in stippled red and sponged blue. At the extreme top left of the whole group is a marbled dark blue frame, followed by frames sporting a variety of decorative finishes, including two rectangles with painted motifs and decoration over white and green stippled backgrounds.

gilded mouldings of the seventeenth and eighteenth centuries.

Most old pictures look best in their original frames but, of course, this is often impossible to achieve, for the original is frequently missing or hopelessly damaged. The search is then on for a moulding that is a modern reproduction of an older look. If possible, the final choice should maintain the original balance: the right proportions between picture and frame, colours that do not clash, and a weight that is not overbearing.

A heavy moulding — a massive look — may be suitable for an image such as a portrait, where the head usually takes up most of the picture surface, but it would be inappropriate for a picture containing many small figures or shapes and a lot of space.

Do not overlook the feelings of the artist. Painters often design and paint the frame as well as the picture. The Pointillist, Georges Seurat (1859–91) extended his 'optical' method of mixing colour used in his pictures to some of his frames, creating a total effect.

It is not easy to decide what sort of mouldings the artist would have wished for a particular painting but some sensitivity and exploration is called for.

Double Frames

Smaller artworks especially can be set off well by double framing, in which a second frame, or 'slip', is inserted within a broader one. The terminology varies but we shall refer to these internal frames throughout the book as 'inserts'.

Why use inserts? They provide a broad ribbon of material between the artwork and the outside world and they do it more gently than would a solid wedge-like frame. The insert provides a gentle transition from the artwork to the outside frame and, in turn, the surrounding environment. More than one insert can be used, giving a multiple frame. They can be made of different materials, can be covered with fabrics such as velvet or canvas, and can be veneered or painted.

The colour and texture of the insert should harmonize with the artpiece, picking up some of its characteristics. A block of dull red in a picture, for instance, can be reflected by a similar colour for the insert. Some purists argue that framers can wrongly emphasize a colour or element in the artpiece by reflecting this in the frame, and certainly with some artworks it may be better to use a more neutral tone,

which does not visually alter the artwork. This is a field in which the framer can have fun learning and experimenting with different effects.

Platform Frames

Another alternative for the smaller artpiece is a platform frame. The artpiece is mounted onto a larger surround, so that it is physically raised up above the surface. The surround can be made of practically any material but wood or cork are favourites, as they allow the picture to 'breathe'.

A VARIETY OF FINISHES

You, too, can paint your own frames, or you can finish them with other materials and techniques. Framers' mouldings are bought ready-finished but builders' mouldings allow you to develop your own artistic talent.

Five basic methods of finishing — waxing, staining, texturing, gilding, and painting — are discussed below with special emphasis on painting, which includes such techniques as marbling and spattering. Details on how to effect these techniques are given on pages 86–97.

Waxing

This finishing technique makes the most of the appearance of the wood itself, whether it is soft or hard. Waxing enriches the natural colour of the wood and also brings out the grain.

Either apply wax straight to the wood surface or use it as a final finish by waxing over another finish, such as staining. Paint the wax on with a brush; several coats can be used and each one should be polished and buffed up with a soft cloth.

For the most effective wax, mix equal parts of melted beeswax, pure turpentine and pure linseed oil. As an alternative to merely enhancing the colour of the wood, you can add your own colouring by mixing wax with artists' oil paint.

Staining

One of the great advantages of staining today is that you are no longer restricted to the traditional, natural colours of wood. Stains are now made in a wide variety of colours and if a shop does not stock exactly the shade you require, mix your own.

Staining preserves the patterns of the wood, simply adding colour. It does leave the wood porous, however, and you will therefore need to seal the finished piece with a wax or varnish.

Some stains are water-based and some spirit-based: be careful not to mix the two types.

Texturing

There are two basic ways of creating a textured surface. You can either cut into the wood, usually with a pointed instrument or 'raking' tool such as a comb, or you can build up a texture by applying certain substances and working on them.

One such substance is a thick coat of paint. Drag

Velvet slip
Traditional materials have been chosen here for a traditional subject. The needlework has been
placed in a mahogany frame with an insert or slip frame which has been covered in rich green velvet.

Applying gold leaf
For both these finishes, begin in the same way by giving the basic frame several coats of gesso and bole. The less expensive method of gilding (left) is transfer gilding, which is bought in the form of gold sheets on a paper backing. Water gilding (below) is an old craft, requiring practice and the right equipment.

a comb or other instrument through the still slightly wet paint to create a pattern. Vinyl paint is particularly well suited to this technique. You can also use gesso, a fine plaster-type finish mixed into a paste from powder and water. Experiment with other materials to achieve interesting or unusual results.

Professional Gilding

Gilding, or 'golding' involves covering the surface with a gold colour or a very fine layer of real gold. For picture frames, the most expensive and difficult method, but also the most professional, is to use real gold leaf. The word 'real' is used here because you can also buy synthetic gold leaf, although this is harder to apply. Real gold leaf is gold beaten into a sheet only 0.0001mm thick. Bought in books or sheets, it is the result of a craft dating back many centuries. Homer's *Odyssey* contains a passage describing how cattle ready for sacrifice had their horns covered with beaten gold. The process of making gold leaf today has changed little since a German monk wrote a basic outline of the technique in the twelfth century.

There are several different types of real gold leaf, all available from art shops. The main ones are named after their countries of origin: English, French and Italian. Although they vary in quality, they all tend to be highly expensive. However, real gold leaf applied well provides a beautiful finish.

Water gilding and oil gilding are the two basic methods of applying gold leaf. With water gilding, the gold is burnished to a very bright finish; with oil gilding, the surface is left matt.

Simple Gilding

There are easier ways of achieving a gilt finish on your picture frame than using real gold leaf. Liquid gold leaf or even gold paint can be used for small areas, such as a narrow band, or for retouching.

Metallic powders are widely available: mix them with a varnish. They are especially good for painting motifs and stencilling patterns but if used for larger areas they tend to look streaky and patchy. Powders can be bought for silver and bronze effects as well as gold.

Another material that can be used for gilding is transfer gold. Similar to gold leaf but easier to apply, transfer gold is a thin layer of gold which is purchased on backing paper. Use it like a traditional transfer, but only for smaller jobs.

Creative finishes
Some wooden frames can be painted so that they resemble different materials, such as the apparent marble (right). The painted golden and auburn tortoiseshell (above) is more obviously stylistic. The effect of wood grain can also be created with paint (above right).

Paint Effects

A wealth of finishes can be obtained with paint, using various tricks to produce different effects.

Paint can be used to achieve a surface that resembles a more expensive texture, such as marble, tortoiseshell, or a rare and exotic hardwood. Once you have learned the techniques, you will be amazed at how easily you can obtain a finish that has the look of a highly professional product. A brief summary of paint techniques follows; for more details on how to effect them, see pages 92–97.

Marbling is the technique of using broken colour to capture the effect of the irregular streaks of the seams in real marble. It rarely actually deceives but marble is accepted today as a legitimate pattern in its own right.

Wood-graining is one of the older crafts. Victorian decorators became skilled at producing the effect of wood grain on furniture and only a few years ago examples of it could still be found in many homes.

Apply a thin layer of paint, so thin that it is transparent, and then carefully drag a dry brush over it to achieve a wavy texture. On top of this, while the paint is still wet, scratch in lines to represent the grains of wood.

Tortoiseshelling makes use of oil-based paint, which is painted into a textured varnish and smoothed out to create the subtly blurred surface of real tortoiseshell.

Rubbing back consists of painting a wet paint onto a dry one of a different colour. Wipe the second colour while it is still wet to leave just a few traces in the grains of the wood. Rubbing back is particularly effective when using gold over a warm colour such as red, or silver over a cool colour or black.

Vinegar painting is sometimes called putty graining. It creates a grain-like pattern but does not attempt to imitate real wood and is most effective when bright colours are used. Any pattern can be pro-

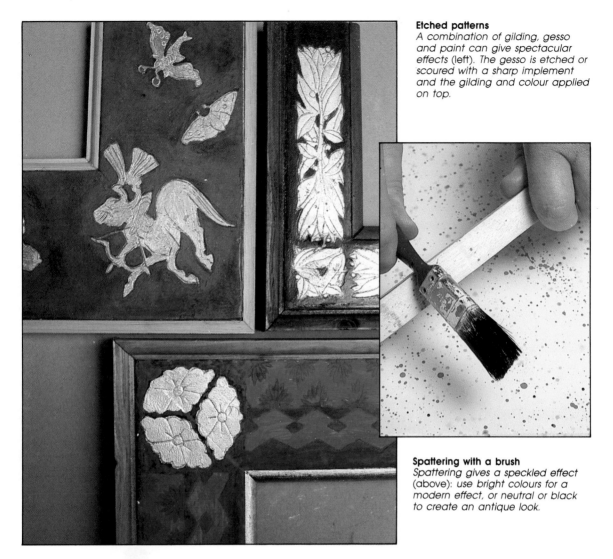

Etched patterns
A combination of gilding, gesso and paint can give spectacular effects (left). *The gesso is etched or scoured with a sharp implement and the gilding and colour applied on top.*

Spattering with a brush
Spattering gives a speckled effect (above): *use bright colours for a modern effect, or neutral or black to create an antique look.*

duced using this technique. Paint one colour onto the frame and allow it to dry. Then paint on a second colour made as a paste from vinegar, sugar, powder colour and a little detergent. While it is still wet, dab it with cork or crumpled paper to make a pattern.

Flicking and spattering require a stiff brush, such as a toothbrush. Run your thumb along the bristles or hit the handle on a strip of wood to spatter the paint onto the moulding. If this is done in a restrained way, using a neutral colour, you can make gilt finishes look old and more subdued. Alternatively, you can let rip and use lots of colours on top of each other to create an exciting effect.

Patinas can be used to create subtle warm and cool tones on the same frame. Begin with a basic pale grey base. Then apply cooler or warmer greys in a thin wash. To make a cooler grey, add blue to the basic grey; for a warmer tone, add burnt sienna or yellow ochre. The best effects are made by mixing warm and cool tones. Apply two or more transparent glazes of warm and cool tones, allowing each layer to dry before applying the next.

Matching the frame to the artpiece can be done with a plain matching colour, matt or gloss, or you can decorate the moulding in a way which is visually sympathetic to the artwork. This is a very old practice: the man generally credited with having discovered oil painting, Jan Van Eyck (1390–1441), is known to have painted his frames to match his pictures. Care is needed, but with flair and imagination frames can be decorated in a way that does not impose an incongruous or overbearing style on the original picture.

Antiquing — making a frame look older and toning down brash colours — can be achieved by using some of the methods mentioned above. Spattering, for instance, if done with black or a dull colour, can tone down a harsh surface. Or rubbing back can be used, again with a dull, neutral top colour.

The Basics of Framing

Materials and Equipment

The Foundation Skills

Finishing Techniques

Materials and equipment

Before you embark on framing a piece, it is essential to become familiar with the parts that make up a framed artpiece and their roles, and to purchase the right tools and equipment. This section takes you through the basic parts of a frame and describes the range of equipment you will need to complete a variety of frames.

PARTS AND FITTINGS

From the outside looking inwards, a framed artpiece is made up of a **rebated moulding**, **glass**, a **mount**, the picture, **inner backing**, and **backing board**. These are all held in position by **veneer pins** and the framed picture is hung with **hanging fittings.**

The names of parts can be confusing as craftsmen have not always been consistent when giving terms to components and techniques. Detailed below are the terms used for a standard glazed frame with a mount and for the fittings that attach it to the wall.

Rebated Moulding

You can purchase moulding with rebate already fitted — ie a stepped moulding — otherwise you will need to buy a separate strip to fit along the bottom of your moulding to make the rebate or 'rabbet'.

The back of the rebated moulding, which rests against the wall, is referred to as the 'bottom edge' or sometimes the 'rebated edge'. The side of the moulding, which you would see if you pressed your eye against the wall and looked at the side of the frame, is called the 'back'. The front edge of the moulding, the strip which the viewer sees, is called the 'front' or 'face'. The edge of the moulding, which overlaps the picture slightly is known as the 'sight edge'.

Glass

The pane of glass used for glazing a picture is usually 2mm ($^1/_{12}$in) thick. A very common commodity, it is stocked by all main glaziers and it can be bought cut to the correct measure if you do not wish to cut it yourself.

Non-reflective glass can also be purchased but this is more expensive and many people feel that it does not give the picture the bright look usually lent by glass but a duller more matt appearance. It is, however, entirely a matter of personal taste and many pictures are framed in non-reflective glass.

Perspex is sometimes used, as this, too, is non-reflective but it is generally not advisable as it scratches easily, becomes static after wiping, attracting more dust, and yellows with age.

Mount

This is a specially made piece of card, which is white all the way through, except for the surface colour. This means that when you cut the bevel to make the window for the picture, you are left with a uniform clean white edge.

Inner Backing

This is the stiff card against which the picture itself is either stuck or held firm in some other way.

If the picture is rare or antique, the inner backing will need to be acid-free conservation board, which is obtainable from specialist suppliers.

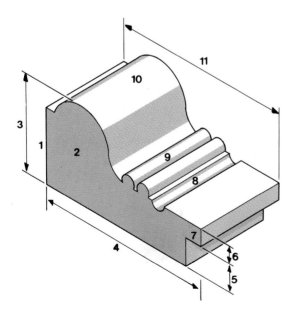

Profile of a moulding
1 *Outside moulding edge*
2 *Moulding profile*
3 *Total moulding height*
4 *Total moulding width*
5 *Rebate*
6 *Moulding inside edge*
7 *Lip of rebate*
8 *Fluting*
9 *Beading*
10 *Ridge*
11 *Moulding face*

Backing Board and Veneer Pins

This is the final backing, usually made of hardboard or craft board and measured to exactly the same size as the glass. After it has been fitted, the tiny gap between it and the bottom edge of the moulding is sealed with brown gum strip as a guard against dust.

When the backing board is lower than the bottom edge of the moulding, it can be fixed into place with veneer pins.

Sometimes the rebate is too shallow to accommodate the glass, the mount and the inner backing as well as the backing board. In this case, the veneer pins are tapped into the moulding and then bent over so that their heads hold the components in position.

If the hardboard is exactly flush with the back of the frame, it can be either bevelled, to allow the veneer pins to be tapped into the moulding at an angle, or it can be held in place with turn clips.

Hanging Fittings

Many different types of fittings are available. Screw eyes, which sometimes have a second ring, are the most common. Such rings are attached directly to the bottom edge of the moulding. Back hangers are useful when a moulding is narrow. These are fixed into the backing board. For bigger pictures with heavy frames, more substantial fittings are required, such as D-rings or otherwise-shaped back hangers. These rings are fitted into a fold of metal, which is screwed into the bottom edge of the moulding.

Fittings are usually fixed a third of the way down the picture. Take care to use picture wire of the correct thickness for the weight of the framed picture.

Wall Attachments

In most cases, a masonry nail is sufficent for hanging a picture, and is easily banged into the wall: place a small piece of Sellotape on the wall before driving in the nail to avoid cracking the wall or paint. If the wall is unusually hard, it may need to be drilled with a masonry drill bit and plugged with fibre or plastic rawlplugs before inserting screws. A large picture can be made more stable by hanging it on two hooks or nails; this also keeps the picture level. If your picture is particularly heavy, it might be necessary to use a bolt that screws into a special casing with an exact fit.

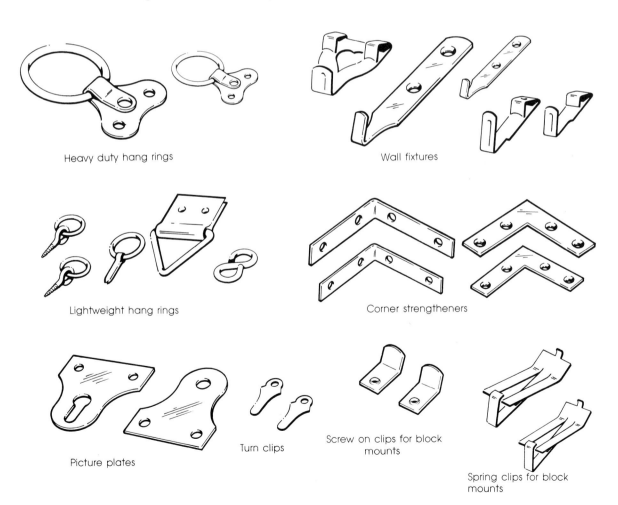

Heavy duty hang rings

Wall fixtures

Lightweight hang rings

Corner strengtheners

Picture plates

Turn clips

Screw on clips for block mounts

Spring clips for block mounts

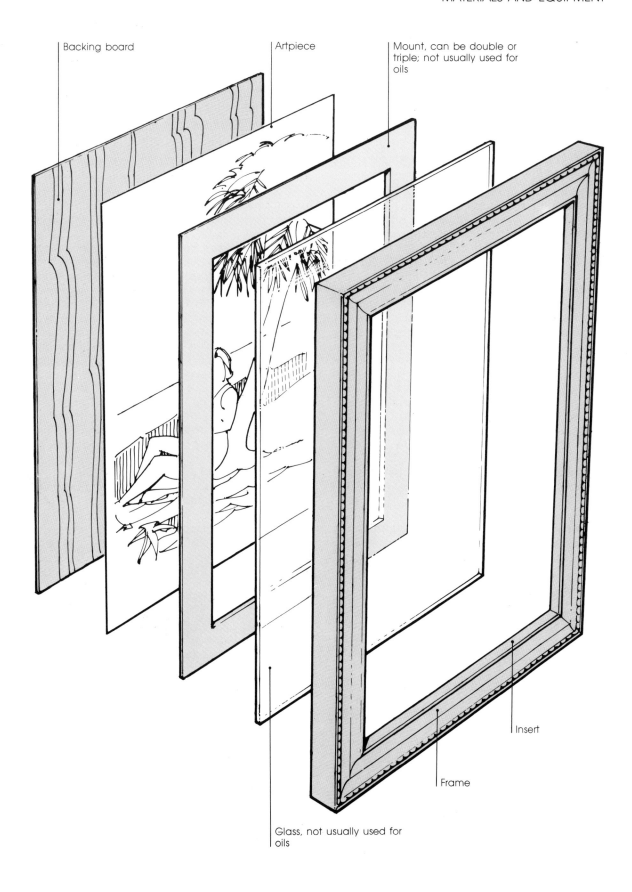

Backing board

Artpiece

Mount, can be double or triple; not usually used for oils

Insert

Frame

Glass, not usually used for oils

DIRECTORY OF TOOLS AND EQUIPMENT

Most professional craftsmen regard with horror the old maxim that only a bad workman blames his tools and advise that no work should be undertaken without tools of exactly the right kind and the proper quality. Even if you are not planning anything elaborate, some good basic tools are essential if the job is to be done well. This directory includes all the basic tools and equipment needed for successful picture framing.

Artists' brushes It is useful to have a selection of these for executing oil and acrylic paint finishes.

Backsaw Also known as a tenon saw. Ordinary saws tend to be flexible and bend; the metal reinforcing strip along the top of this saw prevents the saw blade from 'weaving'. It can be fixed to the workbench with screws.

Bole A red clay pigment used especially in water gilding. Bole is painted on the gesso base to provide a soft, satin-like surface for the gold leaf.

Burnisher Needed to make the smooth, shiny finish so characteristic of water gilding. Most burnishers have an ordinary wooden handle and a curved, smooth metal end which is available in different shapes and sizes for different tasks and is used to burnish the leaf onto the frame.

Carpenters' rule The recommended straight-edge to use when glass cutting. An ordinary thin metal rule is too flimsy to hold the cutter.

Coloured paper Useful for covering mount board if the exact colour of mount board that you require is not available.

Conservation board Sometimes known as 'museum board', conservation board has been treated to rvoid the tendency of ordinary mount board to absorb acid from the polluted atmosphere, which leads eventually to discoloration of the picture. It is advisable to use acid-free conservation board if you are mounting old or valuable drawings or prints.

Craft knife A sharp, general-purpose craft knife, able to cut both card and fabric, is essential for mount cutting. Change the craft blade frequently, especially when you are cutting the bevelled edge of a mount, otherwise the finish will be fuzzy and you will have to trim all the edges.

Decorating brushes It is useful to have a selection of these brushes for waxing, staining and some paint finishes. You will probably not need one more than 37mm (1½in) wide.

Drill Needed to make the pilot holes in the corners of moulding pieces before they are secured together. The most suitable type of drill is a portable household electric drill but a good hand drill is perfectly adequate. Whichever you decide on, you will need a collection of drill bits.

Dry-mounting film Available from graphic suppliers and art shops, this film is placed between the canvas and the backing board and, when heat is applied, fuses the two together.

Dry-mounting press Commercial dry-mounting presses are usually heavy and inappropriate for home framers. Lighter versions are available which are useful if you intend doing a lot of dry mounting; these are basically electric metal presses for use on a table.

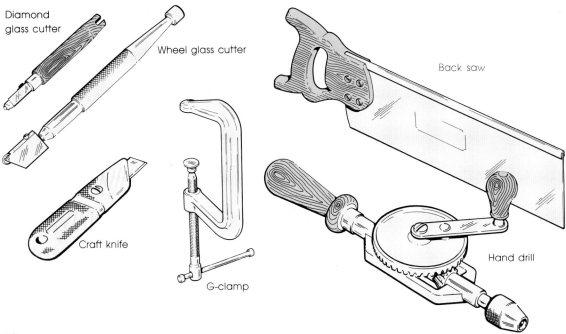

Diamond glass cutter

Wheel glass cutter

Back saw

Craft knife

G-clamp

Hand drill

Face-pieces These scraps of wood are inserted in the vice and screwed to the jaws to prevent the moulding from being damaged by the vice as it is being worked on.

Felt-tipped pen (delible) Can be used to mark the size of the piece of glass required directly onto the glass before cutting. Another method is to draw the cutting lines on a piece of paper, place the paper beneath the glass and follow the lines.

Fitch brushes These are inexpensive and useful for stippling and small-scale decoration and for the spattering effect used in antiquing.

G-clamp If you are making your own rebate, G-clamps (also known as C-clamps) can be used to clamp the moulding to the underlying strip of wood. Also useful as an additional grip.

Gesso A gesso base is needed for both water and oil gilding. Mix gesso powder, which is a chalk, with rabbit-skin glue (both available from art shops) to make the gesso or buy it ready-mixed in fluid form.

Gilders' cushion A padded board covered with suede and used for resting gold leaf. A stiff paper screen boxes in one end of the cushion to protect the gold leaf against draughts: the leaf is so fine and fragile that it can be lifted off the cushion surface by the slightest draught and crumpled, making it unfit for further use.

Gilders' knife This knife has a very fine blade and is used for separating sheets of gold leaf.

Gilders' tip A flat brush with thinly spaced camel hairs, a gilders' tip is stroked across the hand or hair so that it gathers just enough natural oil from the human skin to pick up a sheet of gold leaf from the gilders' cushion.

Glass Picture-framing glass is lighter in weight than normal window glass. It is available in a standard thickness of 2mm ($\frac{1}{12}$in), as opposed to the 3mm ($\frac{1}{8}$in) thickness of window glass or the very thick plate glass used in shop windows, which is sometimes as much as 4mm ($\frac{1}{6}$in) thick.

Glass cutter There are two types of glass cutter. The one that is easiest for the beginner to use comprises a handle with a steel revolving wheel. Most experienced framers, however, prefer the glaziers' diamond, a handle which holds a diamond, which is especially suitable for thin picture glass. Both are used manually and rely upon good measurement and judgement.

Glass-paper Fine glass-paper is needed to rub down the layers of gesso as they are applied in both water and oil gilding.

Graining brush This brush has little tufts of bristles for building up layers of grain effect.

Iron If you do not possess a commercial heat press an ordinary domestic iron can be used for small-scale projects to apply heat in the dry-mounting process.

Metal ruler When cutting a straight edge, either with a knife or mount cutter, a metal ruler is essential. If you use a wooden or plastic ruler, you will pare the ruler's edge. An engineers' metal straight-edge is ideal, if a little more expensive than an ordinary metal ruler.

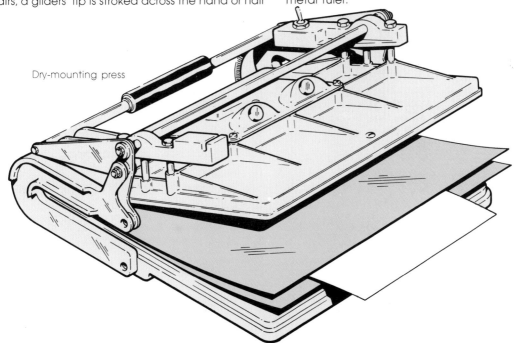

Dry-mounting press

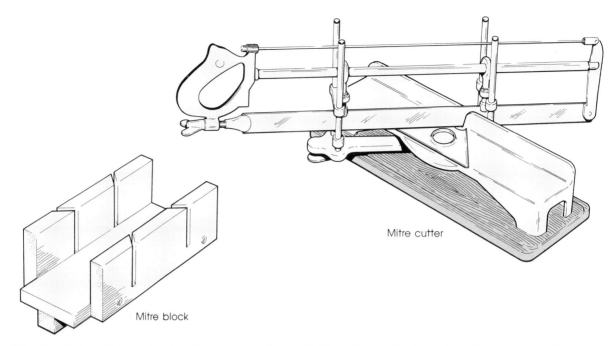

Mitre cutter

Mitre block

Mitre block Essential for forming the corners of a frame, a mitre block must be absolutely accurate. It cuts at an angle of 45 degrees and if it is out of line by even half a degree, the inaccuracy wil be obvious in the finished frame. It is therefore worthwhile buying a good quality mitre block. Unfortunately, a mitre block may become wobbly with use and therefore lose its accuracy. The simplest sort of mitre block is a wooden frame shaped like an open-ended box with slits in each side to guide the saw at a constant angle of 45 degrees. The block is usually made of hardwood but, even so, continuous sawing can wear away the precise measurements of the slits. A more expensive version can be obtained with metal reinforcements at the top of the slits.

Mitre clamp Once the moulding has been cut at right angles for the corners it needs to be held firmly in place so that the pieces can be glued and nailed, and to be gripped in position until the glue has dried. For this, a mitre clamp, made of metal and sometimes called a corner clamp, is used. If possible, the clamp should be fixed by clamping it onto the corner of the table or work-bench to give added stability. A simpler type of corner clamp is made of four plastic right angles which fit around the pieces of moulding and are tightened by a cord. Both types are suitable for simple framing but, for heavier frames, the metal one is easier to use.

Mitre cutter Some of the more sophisticated mitre blocks are made entirely of metal, and the most advanced of all is the mitre cutter which is a mitre box and saw combined in one piece of equipment. These are designed to give absolute rigidity and to prevent the saw from descending too low and causing damage.

Mottling brush Used for breaking up and highlighting the grain.

Mount boards As picture framing has become more popular, an increasingly large choice of mount boards has come on the market. Almost all of them have the traditional distinction of being white throughout their thickness regardless of outer colouring, so that the bevelled edge shows up white. The edge is usually left white but it provides a good base on which to place a gilt strip, or another colour, if you wish. Choice of thickness is usually limited to 4-sheet, 6-sheet and 8-sheet, although thicker card can be obtained or two boards can be stuck together.

Mount cutter This specialist tool cuts the inside bevelled edge of the mount at an angle of 45 degrees. The most useful type of mount cutter has a replaceable blade which is held firmly at an angle and can be set to different depths, depending on the thickness of the mount board.

Oilstone Useful to rub down sharp, newly cut edges of glass.

Paintbrushes Those cut on the diagonal and normally used for painting awkward angles on windows are useful for painting the crevices in mouldings.

Panel pins Fine, round-wire nails from 12 to 50mm ($\frac{1}{2}$ to 2in) long, panel pins can be nailed into the corners of a freshly glued frame to provide a more permanent reinforcement. They have very small heads that can be punched below the surface of the wood.

Mitre clamp

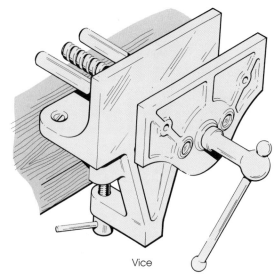

Vice

Rebate plane Also known as a rabbet or fillister plane, it has an adjustable fence, a depth gauge and a cutter that is set in a forward position for planing up to a stopped rebate.

Sable brushes Usually used by watercolourists, sable brushes are useful for fine finishing.

Sandpaper Essential for smoothing a wooden frame before applying a final surface finish.

Shellac varnish Whether you have a gesso or bole final surface, an oil gilding project must be sealed with a coat of shellac varnish.

Set square Essential for drawing accurate right angles when marking out the window in the mount board.

Spray glue Needed in wet mounting to attach the picture to the inner backing as it gives an evenly glued surface.

Table If you do not have a work-bench, a table can be used instead. It must be firm and, if you are setting it up for any length of time, it should be fixed to the floor for extra stability.

Tack hammer A light hammer especially suitable for hammering in the pins and nails used in picture framing. A heavier hammer tends to bend the pins, even if used with care.

Tacking iron For use in conjuction with a dry-mounting press, a tacking iron is like a tiny domestic flat iron but is angled on a handle to enable precision use. It is used to fuse together the picture, dry-mounting sheet and inner backing before final bonding.

T-square Like the set square, a T-square is useful for marking out accurate right angles.

Turpentine When cutting glass, keep the wheel cutter lubricated by frequently dipping it into turpentine or white spirit.

Veneer pins For very lightweight framing, these tiny nails are sufficient to reinforce the corners of the frame.

Vice An ordinary vice can be used to grip pieces of moulding in place while general work is being done on them but its role in picture framing is an all-purpose rather than a specific one. It is also used for drilling and trimming wood, for instance, and should not be confused with the role of the clamp, which is used specifically to hold the corners at rigid right angles.

Wallpaper paste and **water-based glue** Used for wet mounting, although because they are water-soluble they are unsuitable for prints and drawings done in non-waterproof inks.

White spirit Useful for cleaning dirty oil paintings and for lubricating a wheel cutter during glass cutting.

Woodwork glue For glueing the corners of the frame together, a synthetic, PVA-based woodwork glue is most suitable. You do not need to use very much on each corner.

Work-bench Provides a solid and level work surface.

The foundation skills

For oil and acrylic paintings, canvases, hardboard panels or any type of artpiece which cannot be trimmed, the rebate measurement is usually the most useful as it indicates the total ground area, including that which is hidden beneath the rebate. Measure the length and the width of the artpiece and mount, if there is one, and then add 3mm ($^1/_8$in) all round — this allows for easy insertion of the art-piece into the rebate. Many canvases used for oil paintings, especially home-made ones, are 'off-square'. If this is the case, add the extra 3mm ($^1/_8$in) to the longest measurement.

An oil painting is sometimes fitted very snugly into the rebate, almost as far as it can go, inevitably hiding some of the image. If it is important not to cover any of the composition, and the image reaches virtually to the edge of the canvas, then it will be necessary to frame the picture with the smallest possible fraction of it hidden behind the rebate, using spacers to hold it in place, and you will need to take a sight measurement. A sight measurement gives the distance between the inside edges of the front of the frame, indicating precisely the area of the artpiece which will be finally open to view.

WET, OR COLD, MOUNTING

Some drawings or prints are too flimsy to stand by themselves when being placed between backing board and frame, and need to be stuck fast to a rigid support. Glueing a picture to such a board is called wet mounting. Wet mounting is also the quickest and simplest method of block mounting — fixing an artwork to a platform projecting from the surround.

Paintings executed on canvas, which have been removed from their stretchers, can be wet mounted. The technique is also suitable for photographs, drawings, prints and documents and is a good way

Before embarking on specific projects, it is necessary to master the foundation skills of picture framing. These fundamental skills are described below in detail, enabling you to tackle with ease any of the projects that follow.

MEASURING THE ARTPIECE

It is important to take precise measurements whether you are measuring the artpiece, the mount or the moulding. In fact, it is often worthwhile taking a measurement twice to double check.

Before you can calculate the length of the moulding you will need to know one of two basic picture measurements: either the 'rebate' measurement or the 'sight' measurement.

THE PROFESSIONAL METHODS

The professional methods of framing often differ from the basic picture framing techniques. Consequently, throughout this section, in addition to the basic techniques of framing, many of the professional techniques are also illustrated and described in step-by-step format. The professional

techniques covered are those for:

- Wet, or cold, mounting
- Dry, or hot, mounting
- Attaching the window mount
- Cutting a bevelled window
- Cutting an aluminium frame
- Underpinning
- Assembling an aluminium frame

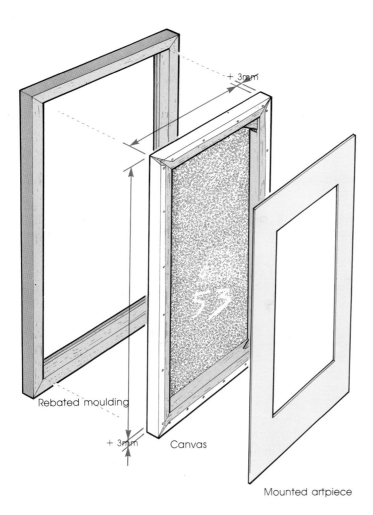

Rebated moulding

+ 3mm   Canvas

Mounted artpiece

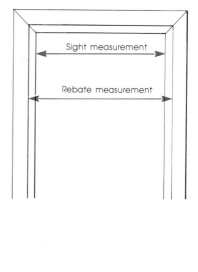

The diagram (left) illustrates the importance of taking accurate measurements. Whether you have a mounted picture or an oil painting on a stretcher, you must fit the artpiece snugly into the rebate of the frame. The diagram (below) clearly shows the difference between the sight and rebate measurements. The sight measurement of a framed artpiece indicates the area of the artpiece open to view. The rebate measurement indicates the total area of the artpiece, including that which is hidden behind the rebate.

Sight measurement

Rebate measurement

of preserving something of sentimental value, which you would not want creased or torn. However, because it is difficult to reverse, wet mounting should be avoided when dealing with antique or rare pictures.

Various types of glue are suitable for wet mounting. An aerosol spray glue is most suitable for pictures done on thin papers and any synthetic glue is suitable for those carried out on thicker paper.

Wallpaper size is often a less expensive and just as convenient alternative. Mix this according to the instructions on the packet but remember that it is water-soluble, so avoid using it on works of art that are printed or painted using water-soluble materials, as traces of it could soak through. If wallpaper size is applied to plywood, it can cause it to warp. When using wallpaper size, remember to 'pre-size' the board: give it a coat of size and allow it to dry. This will seal the board and prepare the surface for the final sizing, resulting in a better grip.

When using a non-aerosol adhesive, it is common to misjudge the amount needed and place too much glue on the backing, so some practice is advisable. To prevent bubbles appearing when mounting a large print or photograph, wet the picture before positioning it on the glued board. Do not

try this, however, with a watercolour or a print effected with water-soluble inks.

When glue and size mounting, flatten the artwork, removing any trapped air, by applying pressure with a roller: roll firmly out from the centre of the picture — a technique also designed to remove any surplus glue. You can ensure that no glue seeps onto the picture by covering it with a sheet of paper before you start rolling. Alternatively, if only a small print is being mounted, or if you do not have a roller, a soft, dry rag can be used: again work outwards from the centre. It is a good idea to weight the picture onto the glued surface while it is drying. This can be done by clamping the picture and mount between two sheets of plywood, or placing them beneath one or two heavy books.

DRY, OR HOT, MOUNTING

Dry mounting is the process of fusing the artpiece to the inner backing by means of heat and a special adhesive sheet. Place the sheet between the picture and the backing and apply the heat. The sheet will melt, fixing the picture firmly on the backing.

If you intend to carry out a lot of dry mounting, it may be worth investing in a press. Place the picture face down on a dry surface while the press is warming up. Position a sheet of mounting tissue — the adhesive sheet — so that it covers the picture's reverse side entirely, and fix the picture and adhesive sheet in position by applying a warm tacking iron along one edge. If more than one adhesive sheet is needed to cover the area, ensure that the edges are butted and do not overlap, otherwise creases and bubbles will mar the result. With each new sheet that is added, apply a tacking iron along one edge to fix it into position.

Trim the edges of the adhesive sheet precisely with a very sharp scalpel or craft blade. Turn the picture and sheet face up and position it on the inner backing. Cover the picture with brown paper and apply the tacking iron again to hold the backing fast along one edge. Place the picture and backing in the press, on top of an extra piece of board for additional stability, and position a sheet of protective paper — usually provided with the adhesive sheet — on top. Close the press and leave for between 30 and 60 seconds to fuse. Remove from the press and place the backing, picture and protective paper under a heavy weight, such as a pile of books.

If you do not have a press, a domestic iron is also suitable both for the tacking and the final bonding. Simply follow the above procedure, substituting an iron for the press. Use a solid, flat working surface and set the iron to 'linen'. Iron out from the centre for the final bonding.

HINGE MOUNTING
In a hinge mount, the inner backing and the mount are hinged together. This keeps the mount board

Spray mounting
The advantage of spray mounting is that it is easy to apply. Place the artwork face down on a clean surface and spray evenly over the back with spray glue (left). Position the artwork on the mounting board—many spray adhesives have a delayed drying time to allow you to adjust the artwork. Smooth down from the centre outwards (below).

Glues for mounting			
Type	**Advantages**	**Disadvantages**	**Drying time**
Wallpaper size	Cheap and strong	Should not be used for valuable items	A few hours to dry properly
Contact glues	Very strong and quick; multi-purpose; can be used on card, rubber, laminates etc	Should not be used for valuable items—once the glued surfaces touch they cannot be pulled apart again.	Instant
Dry mounts	Strong; extremely professional finish	Requires heat	Instant
Spray mounts	Convenient; allows for adjusting and repositioning	Expensive	Up to a few minutes (some have adjustment times)
PVA (can be diluted with water for sticking paper and card)	Can be used on paper, card and fabric, and is very strong		Half an hour to a few hours (depending on type)
Organic glues (including artists' size)	Good for fabrics, card and paper	It goes off; requires gentle heat—can be 'killed' if overheated	A few hours to dry thoroughly
Latex glues	Good for canvas, card, paper etc	Difficult to remove excess; strong smelling	About one hour

PROFESSIONAL METHODS

Wet, or cold, mounting
1 The picture is placed carefully on pressure sensitive film, which is then detached from the rest of the roll.
2 The backing of the film is then peeled off, leaving a strongly adhesive surface. The picture is now ready to place on the backing. Here, craft board has been used as both inner backing and backing board.
3 One end of the print is pressed down on the backing and passed through the rollers of the. mounting press. The rest of the picture is held tautly with one hand against the top roller, while the card and picture is gradually wound between the rollers. In this way, no air bubbles are allowed to form. When the entire print has passed through the rollers, the mounted picture is wound back through the press to ensure that the print is stuck firmly to the board.

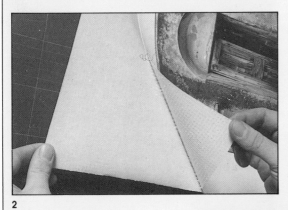

2

3

Dry, or hot, mounting
Dry mounting provides the strongest and most professional-looking bond. The picture is placed face up on dry-mount tissue, which is coated with wax and placed on top of the backing. It is then covered with a piece of clean board to prevent the wax not covered by the picture from sticking to the lid of the press. It is all inserted in the pre-heated dry-mounting press and left for 1 minute to fuse.

Hinge mounts

1 The first stage in the making of a hinge mount is to fix the picture onto a backing. Attach the artwork to the backing with tape, so that it can be adjusted when the window is fitted over it and can also be removed later if necessary.

2 Cut another mount, exactly the same overall size as the first 'backing' mount and cut out a window.

3 Lay the two mounts end to end, and tape them together.

4 Finally, carefully fold the window over the mounted picture.

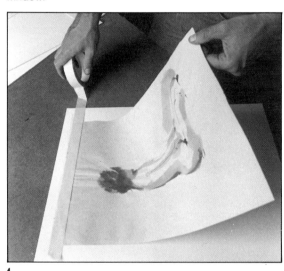

1

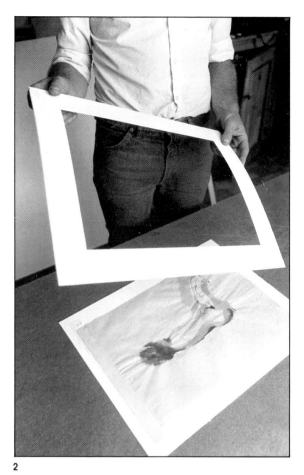

2

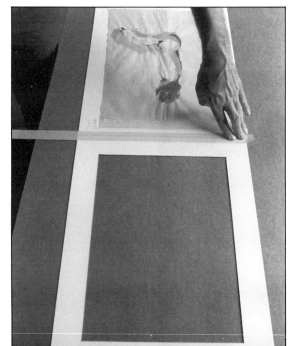

3

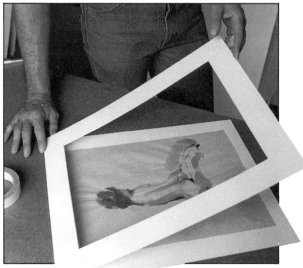

4

1

Attaching the window mount

1 *Double-sided tape is applied to the back of the window along the top and sides, or, if hinge mounting, just to the top edge. The mount is never fixed at both top and bottom as this might result in the picture wrinkling if the picture drops. The mount is then positioned on top of the backing and picture.*

2 *Any additional backing is then cut away with the straight edge of a mount* cutter. *The window mount is used as a guide to leave a clean edge to the mounted picture.*

2

and inner backing together during framing, preventing them from slipping, and allows you to change the artwork and use the same mount over and over again.

To make a hinge mount, cut the window and lay the mount and the inner backing face down on a clean surface, head-to-head with their top edges flush. Then stick the two together, placing a piece of masking tape, gum strip or fabric tape at the top of the backing. Next, fit the picture: determine the exact postition of the picture by trial and error, moving it by degrees behind the window. Then stick the picture onto the inner backing by one of two methods: either affix small pieces of tape to its edges, or, if you particularly do not want the surface of the artwork to be touched by tape, fold over a piece of tape into a little hinge and place it behind the artwork. Double-sided tape can also be used but is not recommended because of its fiercely adhesive quality, which makes precise positioning and removal of the artwork difficult.

CONSERVATION MOUNTING

Although conservation techniques have always been used to help preserve particularly precious artworks, their use has become more common in recent years as attention has been increasingly drawn to the problems of environmental pollution.

Conservation mounting is not simply a matter of isolating the picture from the atmosphere, which contains acid particles and other harmful chemicals. The picture must also be separated from the actual frame, for much of the material used in frame making contains traces of acids which might be damaging to a picture over a long period of time. Acid traces can be found in almost all materials, including cardboard, paper and wood, when they are not specifically acid-free.

Conservation mounting, therefore, involves selecting acid-free materials and ensuring that these, and no others, are placed next to the artwork. Acid-free mounting board, sometimes known as conservation board or museum board, is widely available from specialist suppliers. Acid-free cloth tape can be used to hinge the mounting board to the inner backing and rice paper can be used to stick the artwork to the inner backing. Tear the rice paper into strips, fold into hinges and stick them to the inner backing and artwork with an acid-free glue. Cardboard, especially corrugated cardboard, which is sometimes used as backing, should be avoided when conservation is important: its acid content tends to be particularly high. When you have completed the framing, turn the picture

1

Cutting a rectangular mount

1 *First, decide on the size of the mount: the borders on either side of the artwork should be of an identical width and the bottom border should be wider than the top border. Cut the total area of mount card required from the whole sheet, ensuring that all the corners are square. Now, with a pencil, mark the widths of the borders at several points along each side. Join the pencil dots on one side with a ruler and pencil in a line. Do the same for the other three sides of the window, overshooting at the corners so that you make clear right angles.*
2 *Using a protractor or set square, check that the rules of the window form perfect right angles at the corners. Amend the lines if necessary.*
3 *Place a metal straight-edge along one of the marked lines; tap in two nails at either side of the mount board and rest the ruler against them. Using a sharp craft knife, cut along the straight-edge at*

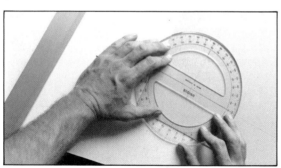

2

4

3

5

6

7

a constant angle of 50 or 60 degrees. Repeat for the other sides of the window.
4 Tidy the corners of the bevelled window with the point of the craft knife blade.
5 The adjoining sides of the window should meet in a clean, precise corner.
6 Rub out any pencil marks that are still visible on the mount.
7 An interesting variation of the standard rectangular mount can be made by 'clipping' the top two corners. Mark the diagonal rules on the mount with a pencil before you begin cutting the bevelled edges.

upside down and seal the back securely with a paper dust seal. To achieve a tight seal between the glass and the frame, pack the backing board, mount, artwork and glass tightly and make the seal firm by tacking nails into the rebate.

MEASURING THE MOUNT

As a rule, the mount is cut first, and then the frame around it, enabling you to position the artwork in the mount. Usually, the sides and the top margins around the mount are slightly narrower than the bottom margin, so that the artwork sits up high in the mount.

Remember that you are beginning with two pieces of card — the backing card and the mount itself. Unless you are using conservation board, the inner backing can be of a cheaper material than the mount. The inner backing and the mount

should be measured and cut so that they both fit neatly into the rebate.

When measuring the window, place the card face down on a clean surface and mark the measurements on the 'wrong', ie reverse, side. Decide the width of the mount surround and mark the margins in as lines on the reverse side of the card. The final window measurement can now be checked with a set square for corner squareness, after which it is ready for cutting.

CUTTING A BEVELLED WINDOW

A bevelled edge — a sloping, rather than straight, edge — gives a professional finish to the window of a mount.

A simple and easily available tool, such as a craft knife, is usually used to cut a bevelled edge, and a metal straight-edge is necessary to guide your

Hand cutting an oval with a knife
It is extremely difficult to achieve a neat, clean edge when hand cutting ovals, so restrict hand cut ovals to mounts that will be covered by paper or fabric.
1 *Using a very sharp scalpel, hold the template down firmly and cut round it.*

1

2 *When you have cut the oval, remove the template and trim any jagged edges. Don't overdo the trimming, however, as this can distort the finished shape.*

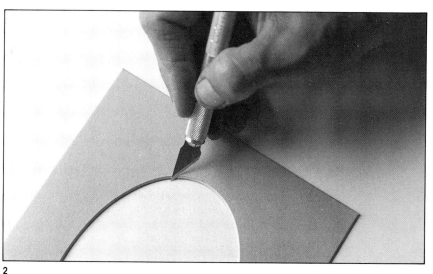

2

hand when you are cutting. The blade used for cutting a bevelled edge must be absolutely razor-sharp. Always keep a supply of spare blades in stock and as soon as cutting becomes slightly difficult, change the blade. Do not use a wooden or plastic ruler, as the knife will shave small flakes from it, not only blunting the blade but quickly ruining the straight-edge and making the ruler unusable.

After measuring and marking out the window, place the card from which it is to be cut face down on a board or table where it won't matter if the surface is cut or damaged. To lengthen the life of your blade, insert newspaper between the card and the board so that you cut into the newspaper rather than the board or table. To prevent the metal straight-edge from slipping while you are cutting, it is a good idea to tap in two nails — one at each side of the mount board — for the ruler to rest against.

With the card still face down, place the ruler along the first marked line to be cut and insert the knife slightly beyond the corner mark outside the window area. This slight overcut — equivalent in distance to the thickness of the card — will not be noticed on the right side of the mount and will ensure that the corners are sharp and precise.

There are two alternative methods for the next part of the procedure, both requiring practice. For the first method, cut along the straight-edge in one smooth stroke, keeping the pressure even, and holding the knife at a constant angle of between 50 and 60 degrees. Cut beyond the corner of the line by the same amount as the overcut at the first corner — the thickness of the card. For the second method, lightly score along the line at the correct angle. Then make another scoring stroke along exactly the same line and at the same angle; repeat until you have cut right through the card. After the first line is lightly scored, you might find it more comfortable to do without the straight-edge.

Repeat the cutting procedure for all four sides of the window. The bevelled edge should be a smooth, clean slope but if you are left with a few jagged

Using a hand cutter

1 *There are several types of hand cutters on the market. This is a Dexter cutter.*
2 *Make straight cuts by placing the cutter against a metal straight-edge.*
3 *Hold the straight-edge very firmly and draw the cutter along, applying a firm, even pressure.*
4 *An oval can be cut in a similar manner, using a template.*
5 *Cutting around a template requires practice as it is difficult to manouevre the cutter at the narrow ends of the oval.*

1

2

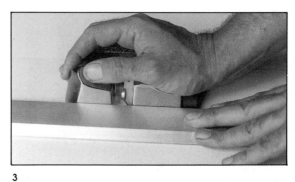

3

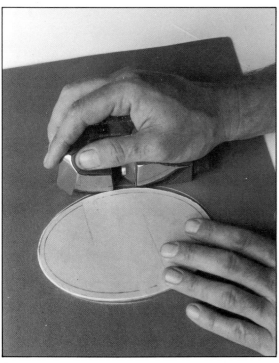

4

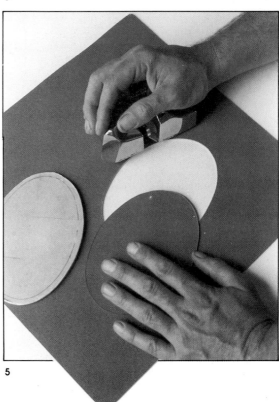

5

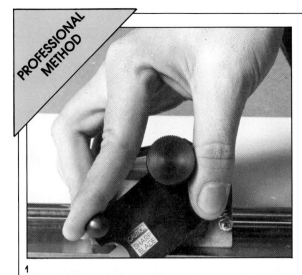

PROFESSIONAL METHOD

Cutting a bevelled window
First the size of the border is determined; the depth of the bottom border is always greater than the depth of the other three, which are usually the same size. Once this is done, the total outside measurement of the window mount is calculated.
1 *Placing the mount card face down and using the straight edge of the mount cutter, the first side of the mount is cut.*
2 *The other three sides are then cut in the same way, altering the stops as appropriate.*

3 *The inner edges are then cut, using the bevelled edge of the mount cutter. A slight overcut is usually made, as this will not show on the right side of the mount and results in the formation of sharp, clean, bevelled corners.*

2

3

pieces, you can often remove them by carefully rubbing them down with very fine sandpaper, glasspaper or emery-cloth.

Some framers recommend using the bevelled edge of the straight-edge to give the hand additional guidance although, since it is the hand itself that maintains the angle, this method still requires practice.

APPLYING LINES AND WASHES

To decorate the mount, lines can be drawn around the window and some of these filled in with washes. For an especially rich look, strips of gold are also applied. The number of lines, their thickness and spacing are important if you wish to avoid an over-fussy appearance and it is advisable to lightly pencil the lines around the window before applying the wash, measuring up in order to keep them strictly parallel.

A typical line-wash mount consists of a ruled line 6mm (¼in) to 12mm (½in) from the bevel, followed by a broader band of wash and enclosed by an outer double line. Ideally, the colour of the wash

and lines should echo some of the colours in the picture without swamping the image. Generally, bright colours should be avoided because they detract attention from the picture. If you particularly wish to use a strong colour, such as viridian or magenta, try muting them slightly, without drastically changing them, by mixing a tiny amount of a complementary colour with them. Black may seem an obvious choice for the lines but, on the whole, is better avoided, as the starkness of black dominates a light-coloured mount too much and dark browns, greens or blues are preferable.

Before applying the wash, it is a good idea to wet the area between the lines, lightly wiping it with a soft watercolour brush dipped in water. The colour will then flow onto the paper without leaving unsightly tide marks. Apply the colour in several thin layers, until you achieve the required colour density for your mount.

When the wash is completely dry, define the coloured area with a stronger outline, using a ruling pen; usually the line is drawn in a deeper tone of the wash colour. Wait until this line is completely dry

Lines

Before applying lines and washes, mark off all the measurements from the window outwards (left). Mark these guidelines in light pencil all the way round the mount, or mark dots at the corners, or make pin holes if the line is to be particularly fine. Lines can be drawn with ruling pens, rapidographs, felt-nibbed pens, pencils or even crayons. A combination of different thicknesses and textures is usually more interesting than a regular arrangement.

Using a ruling pen

A ruling pen has an adjustable nib, allowing you to alter the thickness of the line. The pen can be filled by dipping it into the ink (below), but if you do this you must clean the edges afterwards. Alternatively, load a brush with ink and fill the nib from this. Draw a line against a ruler (right), making sure that the ruler is upside down so that its bevelled edge (bottom) creates a space, preventing the ink from touching the ruler directly.

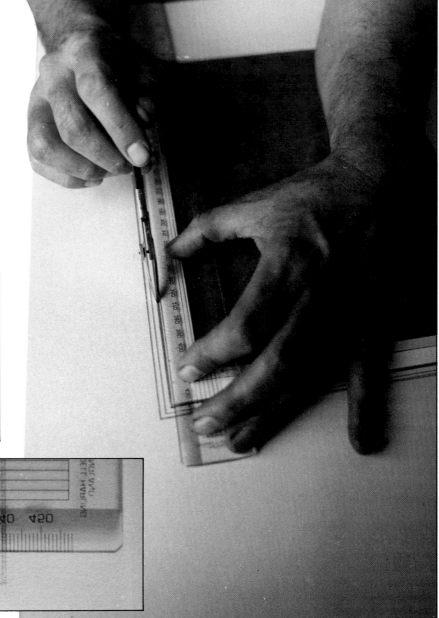

Washes

Use pencil lines to guide you when applying lines and washes to mounts. As a guide for the washes or to the finished lines themselves, draw lightly with a pencil against an ordinary Perspex ruler (right). You can then apply gouache freehand with a brush (below). Make sure the gouache is thin but creamy enough to be opaque.

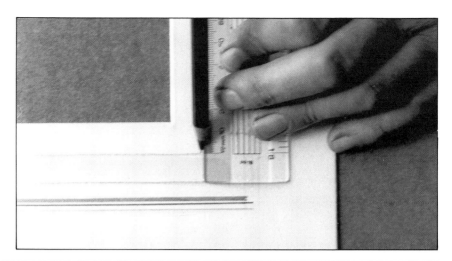

Wash and line

All these washes and lines can be done by the home framer (left to right): silver and light grey on a dark background; sepia lines and a pale wash on white; black line and wash on medium; black, gold and white on light; compact white and dark on medium.

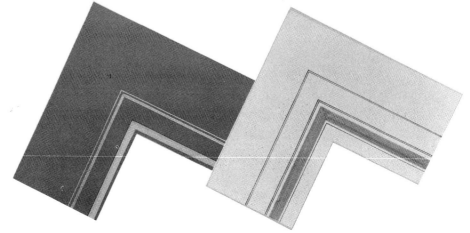

Types of line
Apply a line to a mount, using a gold pen (left). Lines can be drawn along the edges of a strip of wash to tidy it up, or they can be drawn first and a wash applied between them with a brush. They can also stand alone, in varying widths, if desired.

Wavy lines
Sometimes a wavy or irregular line can look attractive amid all the straight verticals and horizontals of the frame, the picture and the mount (above). Another attraction of wobbly lines is that they are easier to create than perfectly straight ones!

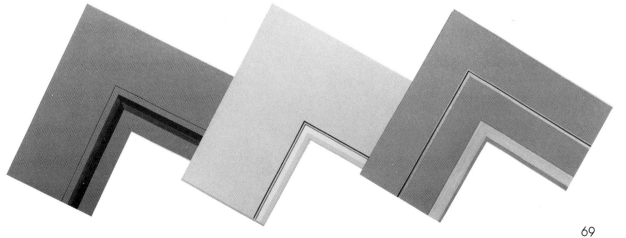

before adding any other border lines, otherwise you may cause smudges with your hands, spoiling hours of painstaking work.

Use the bevelled edge of a ruler to draw lines: place the ruler upside down on the mount, leaving a tiny gap between the paper and its raised edge so that the ink or paint will not blot should the colour come into contact with the edge of the ruler.

Ordinary dip pens can be used to draw the lines but they are not very reliable, and by far the best way to achieve a continuous straight line is to use a ruling pen. Turn the knob on the side of the nib to adjust the width of the line but remember that the nib holds a limited amount of ink, so that a very wide line must necessarily be a very short one, as the colour will run out very quickly; it is difficult to continue a broken-off line in a smooth fashion.

Gold and silver inks are more difficult to use than ordinary inks or watercolours: they are not so evenly mixed and can form sediments, making it harder to achieve a smooth flow. It is often a better idea to buy metallic gummed strips, which can be cut to the required width. However, some of these are rather bright and care should be taken not to overdo the banding or the effect will be too brash.

COVERING THE MOUNT

Once the window has been cut, the mount can be covered with fabric. This is generally a better idea for oil paintings and heavier works than for water-colours.

The easiest method of covering a mount is to cut a piece of cloth slightly larger than the whole mount: glue this to the mount and then cut a window from it in such a way that flaps can be folded over to complete the covering. This method can be used with any shaped window, including round and oval ones. Use a spray adhesive for sticking the fabric to the mount.

CALCULATING THE LENGTH OF THE MOULDING

To work out the exact total length of moulding that will be required, first add together the length and

Fabric-covered mounts
When cutting fabric to cover a rectangular mount, allow enough material to fold over the edges. Cut slots into the inside and outside corners (right), so that they will fold back neatly. Place the fabric face down on a clean surface and spray on adhesive.

To discover the total length of moulding you will require, measure the length and width of your artpiece, multiply the total by two and add 12mm (¹/₂in) for an easy fitting margin. Next, measure the width of the moulding and multiply this figure by eight to allow for the mitred ends.

width of your picture and mount, if there is one, using the rebate measurements (see page 56) and multiply the total by two. Next, to take account of the moulding that will extend beyond the picture at the corners of the frame, measure the width of the moulding you have chosen and multiply this figure by eight. Add this to the first (picture) figure. This gives you the total length of moulding needed.

CUTTING THE MOULDING

When cutting framers' moulding into separate pieces it is important to avoid confusion by working always from the back edge, ie from the edge of the strip which contains the rebate and from the same end of the strip. It is also important to make one side of the frame at a time rather than trying to measure up the whole strip for cutting.

Cutting a Mitre

Once you have determined the entire length of the moulding that you require to frame your art-

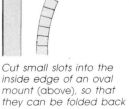

Cut small slots into the inside edge of an oval mount (above), so that they can be folded back in a curve.

Cutting a mitre
1 *Place a piece of moulding face up in a mitre box to make the first cut. The rebate edge of the moulding fits up against the inside edge of the mitre box.*

2 *If you are using a metal mitre box, it can also be used as a corner clamp in the later glueing and nailing stage.*

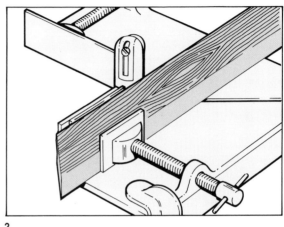

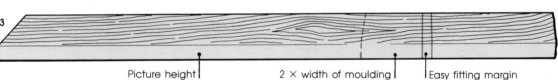

Picture height | 2 × width of moulding | Easy fitting margin

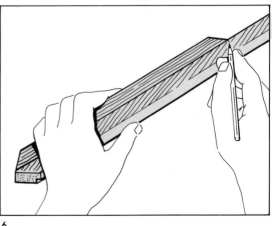

3 *Place the moulding face up and measure it from the longest edge of the mitre.*

4 *Mark the outside edge of the frame with a pencil. Line up the pencil mark with the cutting channel of the mitre box and saw, making sure that the saw cut is on the waste side of the moulding.*

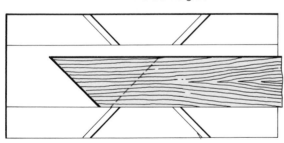

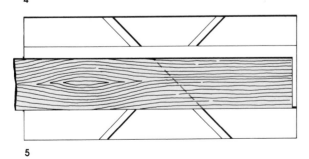

5 *Place the remaining piece of moulding in the mitre box and cut the first mitre of the second strip.*

6 *Measure off the length of the second piece. Use the first piece as a guide, placing them back to back.*

piece, your first task is to cut a mitre at the end of the strip. A mitre is the joint of two pieces of wood at an angle of 90 degrees, with the line of the junction exactly bisecting this angle. Precision is vital when cutting a mitre: if the angle on one of the pieces is even slightly off 45 degrees, you will finish with a gap at the corners of the frame where the two pieces of moulding should meet exactly. It is important to rule out the possibility of cutting a mitre by simply measuring the angle and cutting the moulding freehand. You would have to be extremely lucky to succeed in cutting a perfect mitre using this method. A mitre box or a mitre cutter is essential.

Place one end of the moulding in the mitre box, making sure that the back of the moulding is absolutely flat on the bottom, the rebate edge is nearest to you, and the strip is flush with the sides of the box. If you are using a metal mitre box, place a thin batten of wood between the moulding and the edge of the box, so that the metal does not mark the wood. If you are using a metal mitre box and a saw is not built into it, use a backsaw with it: the manufacturers will recommend the most suitable one. A wooden mitre box is less expensive than a metal one and is used with a tenon saw, preferably one with a thin blade. The mitre box will guide the action of your saw precisely. Use a slow, easy cutting motion rather than a fast energetic one, which will cause the saw to turn and twist.

Now mark out the first total measurement — picture height plus twice the width of the moulding plus easy-fitting margin — starting from the mitred end. There is no need to mark any other measurements on the strip at this point as the second strip will be cut based on the first length. Remove the moulding from the mitre cutter and lay it down with the rebate upwards. Mark the measurement on the outside edge of the moulding. Then replace the

Using a metal mitre box
1 *This metal mitre box has holes in its base so that is is not restricted to cutting angles of 45 degrees. Place pieces of dowling in the holes to allow you to change the angles for frames of more complex shapes.*
2 *Whatever type of mitre box you use, always clamp it firmly to the work-table. Here, the framer has chosen to use a G-clamp.*
3 *Hold the moulding firmly in position with one hand. The metal guides keep the sawing at a precise angle to ensure a perfectly fitting corner.*

The Marples mitre box

A popular model, the Marples mitre box is a simple tool, which can be used as a corner clamp as well as a mitre cutter.

1 Hold the box in position on the work-table with a G-clamp.

2 Insert the wood into one of its sections and tighten the screws to hold it in place while the mitre is cut.

3 Place the tenon saw into its guides, holding it firmly.

4 Use a good quality saw and keep the sawing action steady for a clean cut.

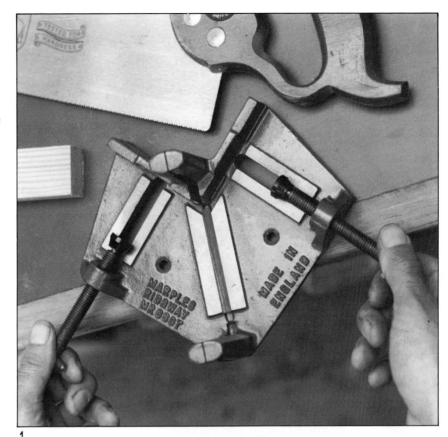

1

2

3

4

Variety of angles
1 *This more complicated mitre box has a protractor fitted to it, which allows the user to cut a wide variety of angles to create triangles or otherwise shaped frames.*
2 *It contains its own saw.*
3 *Set the saw carefully at the appropriate angle.*
4 *Hold the wood firmly in place against the metal support.*
5 *You will then be able to make an accurate cut with the saw.*
This mitre box, like the others, is clamped to the work-bench by G-clamps. Make sure that it is securely held before setting angles and making cuts.

1

2

3

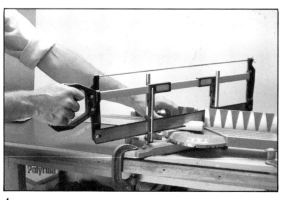

4

5

moulding in the mitre cutter, with the mark in line with the channel of the cutter. This means that the mark is directly beneath the saw blade which will cut diagonally through the point to produce your second mitre. You now have the first complete side of your frame.

You will now find that the remaining piece of moulding already has a diagonal cut at one end, left over from the cut which created your first complete side. However, this is obviously facing the wrong way and, as an initial step to your second complete side, it is once again necessary to cut a first mitre, from this same end. Next, place the complete side back to back with the remainder of the strip, putting the mitre cuts together so that they are completely flush. Now to mark a diagonal line across the uncut strip, using the end of the first side as a guide. Place the uncut strip in the mitre cutter

and cut along the marked line to produce a second identical side for your frame.

Repeat this procedure for the other two sides of the frame, substituting the picture width measurement for the picture height measurement.

FORMING THE CORNERS

When joining two pieces of moulding, first place them back to back to ensure that they are exactly the same length.

Using a Vice

Place one piece of moulding in the vice and, if you are right-handed, hold the other piece in your left hand, keeping your right hand free to work with. Apply woodworkers' resin adhesive to the sawn-off mitred end of the length of moulding held in the vice and hold the mitred end of the other piece

PROFESSIONAL METHODS

1

Cutting a wooden frame
1 The strip of wooden moulding is placed in the mitre cutter, face up, with the outside edge towards the operator. Supports are wedged under the rebate so that the descending blades do not crush it. The extra amount of moulding required to accommodate the mitred ends is then calculated and allowed for and the machine operated.
2 The blades descend on the moulding to cut out a triangle of wood. The cutter is then released. The cutter is worked several more times, each time cutting a little deeper. By cutting through the wood gradually in this way, the moulding is not crushed and two perfect mitres are created. The first length of the frame is then removed from the cutter and the rest of the strip moved along so that the next mitres can be cut and the second length of frame completed.

2

Cutting an aluminium frame
The strip of metal framing is placed in the metal mitre cutter, with the outside edge facing the operator. The machine allows for the extra length needed to accommodate the mitered ends. The blades slice through the framing, leaving two precise miters.

firmly against it. Using an electric drill with a 1½mm (¹/₁₆in) drill bit, make two pilot holes across the join, always ensuring that the drill passes right through into the second piece of wood; it is vital to hold the pieces firmly together so that there is no slipping as you drill. Now drive size 18 panel pins, 18mm (³/₄in) long, into the pilot holes and release the left-hand piece of wood, which is now fixed to the moulding held in the vice. To achieve a neat finish, counter-sink the pins, using a nail punch to drive them slightly below the surface, so that the hole can be filled with plastic wood filler.

If you do not have a drill, it is best to leave the glue to harden in the join before making a hole with a bradawl and nailing the pieces together. Modern rapid-dry glues set in half an hour to an hour.

Using a Clamp

If you have a mitre clamp, sometimes called a corner clamp, instead of a vice, the task is made slightly easier, as the clamp holds both pieces together at rigid right angles, leaving both hands free to insert the panel pins after glueing.

Glues for Framing			
Type	**Advantages**	**Disadvantages**	**Drying times**
Scotch glue (organic glue available in flakes or sheets	Set glue can be heated to dissolve making it possible to correct mistakes	Time consuming and brittle; not as strong as PVA	Overnight
PVA	Convenient; no heat needed; very strong	Cannot break and re-set	Half an hour to overnight (depending on use and type)
Epoxy resins (there are several of these including Araldite and the 'super glues'	Set quickly; very strong	Cannot break and re-set; spills and drips cannot be removed once set	Few minutes to an hour

1

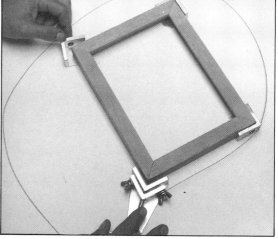

2

Cramping methods
1 As an alternative to using corner clamps (or cramps), a vice can be used, as long as it can accommodate two pieces of wood. Glue the mitred ends and place the two pieces together. Then make holes for nailing with a bradawl.
2 Another method of clamping is to use an Elwood clamp. This consists of four metal corners, one of which has a screw attached. Run wire around the notches in the corners and tighten with the screw. **3** With the frame held firmly in place while the glue is drying, drill holes for the nails.

3

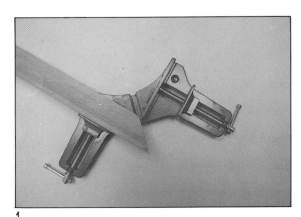

1

Corner clamps

1 *For lighter frames, corner clamps are useful. Fit the first piece of mitred wood into one side of the clamp.*
2 *Glue the second piece and place it into the clamp.*
3 *Ease the pieces together, making sure they are flush. Then tighten the clamp and wipe off any surplus glue.*
4 *If you are making a deep box frame, you may find that the clamps hold* the bottom firmly but do not apply sufficient pressure to the top. In this case, position metal spring clips on the corner with pliers that first hold them apart and then release them onto the corner.*

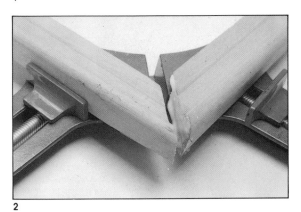

2

3

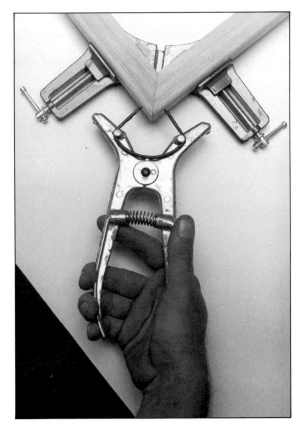

4

Checking corners

Lightweight clamps do not automatically make a precise right angle. Make the two 'L-shapes'. Then check the corner of the first two pieces (above) before fixing them together to form a rectangle.

PROFESSIONAL METHOD

Underpinning
1 The mitred ends of two sides of the frame to be joined are glued together and then placed face up in the underpinner. The machine is operated and a staple is forced up into the wood across the join. 2 The underpinner is worked several times along the join to ensure that the corner of the frame is made secure.

1

2

CREATING A REBATE

Framers' moulding comes with a fitted rebate but if you buy builders' moulding you will need to make your own rebate — the 'step' beneath the frame itself into which the picture fits.

There are two basic ways of creating a rebate. One method is to fix a wooden strip onto the moulding before you begin cutting the mitres. This piece of wood is called a quadrant and comes in a variety of sizes and woods. The other method is to make, in effect, two frames and then fit them together: the broader, top rectangle is the frame itself; the narrower one fits at the back to form the rebate.

Using a quadrant

Select a strip of builders' moulding and fix a rebate strip to the back of this before you begin measuring the specific lengths and mitring the ends. Glue one side of the rebate strip. Lay it flush with the outside edge of the moulding and fix it from the back of the rebate edge with panel pins. You have now made your own framers' moulding and are ready to measure it and cut the mitres.

Making two frames

Begin by cutting the two shorter rebate strips: measure the width of the artwork and add 3mm (⅛in) to allow for easy fitting. This margin is particularly important when you frame canvases, as they are often a shade off-square and their corners are frequently bulky. Next cut the two longer strips:

measure the length of the artwork and add 3mm (⅛in) plus twice the width of the strip. This method will allow the shorter strips to be fitted inside the longer ones. You do not need to cut mitres on these rebate strips as the rebate will be stuck behind the frame and therefore does not need neat cornering.

Now cut the strips of moulding for the outer frame. The ends of these strips must be mitred *(see pages 70–75)*. When cutting the top rectangle, remember that its final outer boundary — the measurement of all its outside edges — should be exactly the same length as the outer boundary of the rebate rectangle so that when the two rectangles are fitted together, their outside edges will be flush with each other. The outer frame must overlap the inner edges of the rebate rectangle to form the 'step' into which the picture will fit.

Next fit the pieces together, starting with the rebate pieces. Apply glue evenly over the whole cut surface of the end of one of the shorter pieces. Then hold the glued end against the end of the inner side of one of the longer rebate strips using a corner clamp or a vice to help the adhesive form a strong bond. Tap two panel pins into the end of the join to give extra stability. Repeat this process on all the corners, working in such a way that you produce two L-shapes, and finally join them both together to make the inner rectangle. Follow the same procedure with the mitred strips of wood to form the outer rectangle of the frame.

When the glue is dry, stick the two rectangles

Making a rebate
Rebates can be cut into pieces of moulding with a plough plane (right). It is fitted with a steel depth gauge and an adjustable 'fence', which can be set to the width of the rebate required. Alternatively, stick a wooden strip, or quadrant, (below) along the length of a piece of moulding.

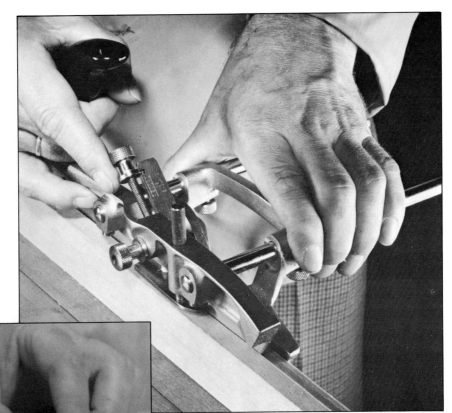

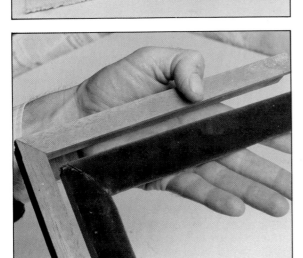

Covering an insert
When making an insert, make sure you completely cover the front and the rebate with fabric, so that no bare wood will show when it is fitted into the main frame (above).

together. Lay the rebate rectangle flat and cover the whole of its top surface with adhesive. Place the outer rectangle face down and place the rebated rectangle adhesive-side down on top of the outer one. Fix it in position with panel pins. Make sure that the surface on which you are working is absolutely clean to avoid marking the front of the frame.

COVERING A FRAME INSERT
Strips of fabric are usually sufficient to cover wooden inserts. As inserts are made from strips of moulding which then fit inside the outer frame, it is possible to cover the separate strips of insert moulding before joining them together. If you do follow this method, the corners of the insert will be neat because the fabric will be glued between the joins.

Alternatively, you can cover the insert after it is assembled. Glue on strips of cloth and then mitre the corners with a very sharp blade. The advantage of covering after assembly is that you avoid the difficulty of keeping the fabric clean while assembling the frame insert.

GLAZING
When your frame is completed, you may well wish to place the artwork beneath glass. For many frames, the procedure for cutting glass can be satisfactorily carried out at home, although any work involving glass must be completed extremely carefully.

Cutting very large pieces of glass, however, is best left to the expert: large pieces are difficult to carry; a

1

3

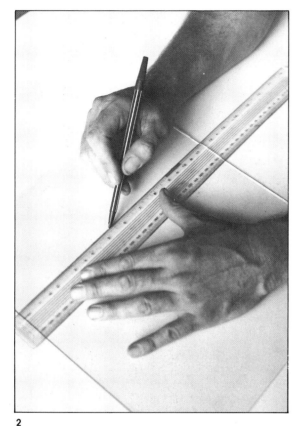

2

Cutting glass

1 There are two basic types of glass cutter. The most common type has a small tungsten carbide wheel. The other, a diamond glass cutter, is used mainly for thicker glass.
2 Use a ruler and felt-tipped pen to mark where you are going to cut the glass.
3 Keep the glass cutter lubricated by dipping it into special glass-cutting oil, a thin mixture, or methylated spirits.
4 To score a line, hold the ruler firmly in place and keep the glass cutter vertical. This requires practice: too little pressure makes no impression at all and too much cracks the glass.
5 Tap the glass along the scored line with the knob on the end of the cutter.
6 Make the final snap by breaking the glass over the edge of a table.
7 If you are cutting a small section you can break it with glass pliers by placing the scored line along a table edge and giving the glass a sharp tweak.
8 Alternatively, break the glass by placing the scored line over the edge of a ruler.

suitable surface may be hard to find for a large operation; and the bigger the frame the greater the chance that your rebate will be inaccurate.

The glass must fit very tightly inside the frame — it should not slip around inside the rebate. Moreover, if the glass is a shade too big when cut, there is little you can do to rectify matters, although, occasionally, it may be possible to sandpaper it down to size. Measuring and cutting must, therefore, be very accurate and the allowance for easier fitting should ideally be no more than 1mm ($^1/_{20}$in).

To enable you to avoid accidents with fragile picture glass it is advisable to practice glass cutting. Repeatedly cutting waste pieces of glass will increase your confidence and accuracy and it will also give you a good idea of the correct pressure that should be applied when cutting.

The surface on which you cut the glass should be completely level and non-slip. Use double-sided tape to prevent the glass and your straight-edge from moving.

Measure and mark the glass, preferably with a felt-tipped pen so that any wrong marks can be rubbed out with white spirit if necessary. (Although, if you do leave any measurement marks, they are likely to be covered up in the last instance because the edges of the glass will be fitted under the rebate.)

The next stage is the actual cutting: the object is not to cut through the glass completely but to score it, so that is can be snapped cleanly along the line. Place the straight-edge along the felt-tip mark and pull the cutter towards you with a pressure that is firm but not so firm that it cuts right through the glass. The scored line should pass cleanly over the edges of the sheet. Score the glass once only; twice makes little difference and can damage the cutting wheel even if you are using a tungsten carbide

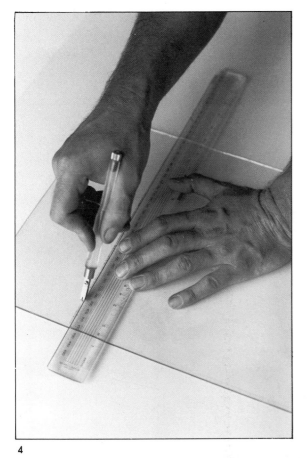

4

5

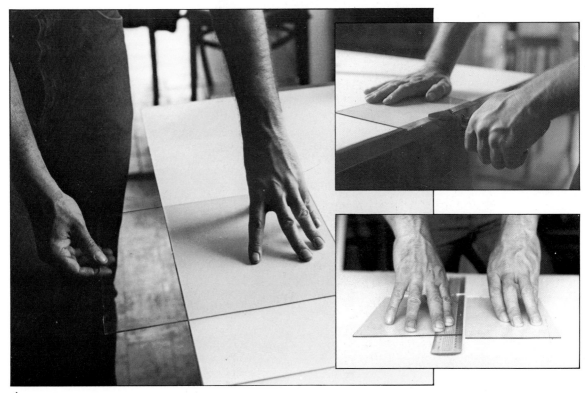

6

THE BASICS OF FRAMING

wheel, which is superior to and much longer-lasting than an ordinary steel wheel.

There are several ways of snapping the glass. Most glass cutters have knobs on the end, which allow you to tap the glass along the cut: tapping gently but frequently ensures a clean snap. Another method of snapping is to slide the straight-edge beneath the glass, almost up to the score line but just to the immediate left of it. Then, when you press down on the right-hand side, the glass will snap, leaving a clean edge. Another method is to lift the glass slightly with your left hand (if you are right-handed), placing your thumb and first finger, with thumb on top, over the edge of the glass just to the left of the score line. Then take hold of the glass with

your right hand just to the right of the score line. With one quick downward movement of your right hand the glass will snap.

Finishing, if required, can now be carried out by rubbing the edge of the glass with wet emery paper.

Remember that throughout the whole operation it is necessary to keep the glass cutter lubricated by frequently dipping it in white spirit.

ASSEMBLING

Always work from the back of the frame and make sure that the surface on which you are working is clean. First insert the glass into the rebate, making sure there is no dirt on it. Then insert the picture and

Assembling the frame
*When assembling all the components, remember to work from the back.
With the frame held face down, fit the glass into the rebate at the rear. Then fit the mounted picture, followed by the backing board, if this is being used. The oil painting and frame (right) are ready for assembly. Bradawl, steel tacks and hammer are necessary to secure the painting.*

82

Using tacks
Ordinary steel tacks can be used to hold the components in place. After the frame has been assembled, tap the tacks into the inside edges of the main frame (left). One *on each side should be enough to hold the frame together.*

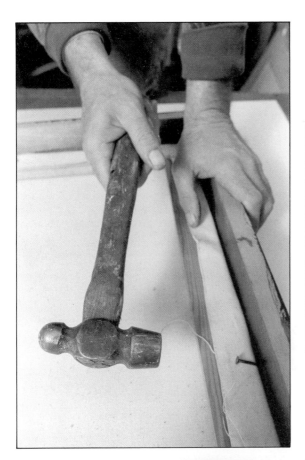

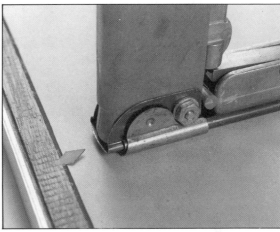

Using a point-driver
An alternative way of securing the components is to use a point-driver (above). Holding the machine down firmly onto the back of the *assembled parts, pull the trigger to send a diamond tack into the inside edge of the main frame.*

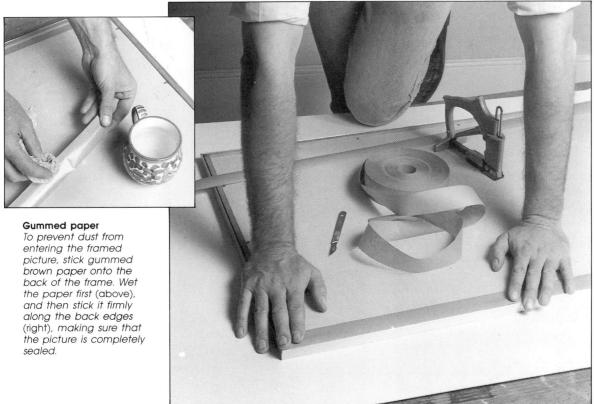

Gummed paper
To prevent dust from entering the framed picture, stick gummed brown paper onto the back of the frame. Wet the paper first (above), and then stick it firmly along the back edges (right), making sure that the picture is completely sealed.

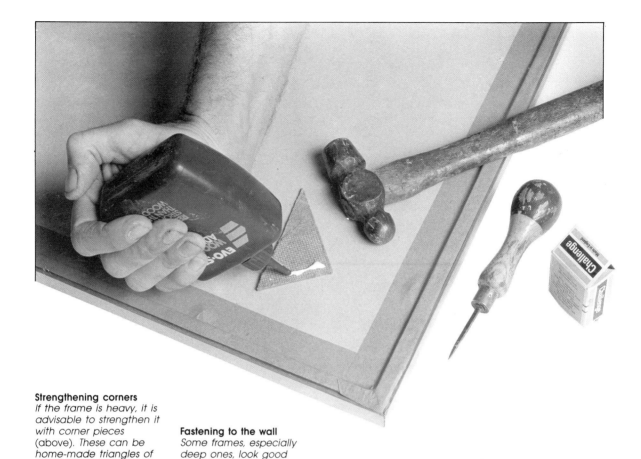

Strengthening corners
If the frame is heavy, it is advisable to strengthen it with corner pieces (above). These can be home-made triangles of hardboard. Glue and then tack them into place on the back corners of the frame. Make sure that they are placed so that they are not visible from the front.

Fastening to the wall
Some frames, especially deep ones, look good when screwed up flat against the wall. Fastening plates can be bought for this (right). For hanging most framed pictures, screw-eyes and wire are ideal (below right).

mount, if there is one, face down on the glass. Finally, insert the backing board. There are several ways of holding everything in place. If the rebate is deeper than the thickness of all the parts, hammer veneer pins into the rebate, behind the backing board, at intervals of 5cm (2in). If the parts are thicker than the rebate, hammer the veneer pins into the back of the frame and bend the heads over the backing board. If the backing board lies flush with the back of the frame, it is a good idea to hold everything in place with turn clips. Once everything is assembled, seal the edges with strips of brown gummed tape. This prevents any dust from entering.

HANGING

Using a bradawl, punch a hole either side of the frame about a third of the way down. Screw in screw eyes. Then run picture-framing wire through the eyes, knotting it at either end with pliers. Take care not to leave the wire too taut. Finally, wind the spare ends back round the wire.

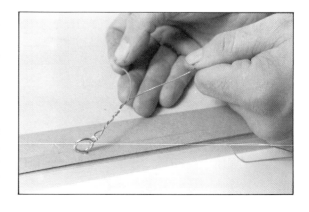

PROFESSIONAL METHOD

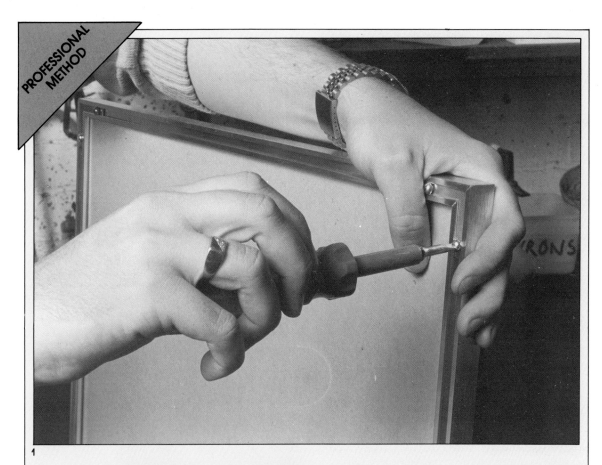

1

2

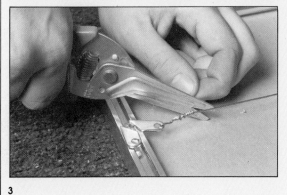

3

Assembling an aluminium frame

1 Chevrons are placed on either end of the top strip of the frame and screwed into place from the back. The two adjoining strips are then inserted into the chevrons and also screwed into place. The picture, backing and glass are then slid into the frame and the final side of the frame screwed into place.

2 Springs are inserted between the backing board and the back of the frame towards the corners to keep the picture pressed against the glass.

3 Two butterfly clips are inserted into the frame a third of the way down each side of the picture. These are then turned and knocked firmly into place. Wire is then threaded through one butterfly clip and twisted round on itself. Any extra wire is clipped off with a wire cutter. The wire is threaded through the other clip in the same way and the picture is ready for hanging.

Finishing techniques

Finishing the frame provides an ideal opportunity for experiment. You can transform the bare appearance of builders' moulding in a wide variety of ways by choosing any of the following basic finishing techniques and adapting them to your own personal taste. Remember to bear in mind the type of artpiece you are framing when deciding on the finish.

APPLYING GESSO

To create a perfect finish, it is advisable to treat the wood surface with gesso before painting or gilding it. This prevents paint or size from sinking into it and also provides a fine, smooth surface on which to apply the final touches.

Gesso is a fine white powder, rather like plaster of Paris, and is available from art shops (full instructions are provided with the product). Work the white gesso powder into rabbit-skin glue to a thin, milk-like consistency; brush onto the surface and allow to dry. Apply a second coat and, when it is dry, lightly rub it down to achieve a completely smooth finish.

GILDING WITH REAL GOLD LEAF

Gilding is the technique of placing a fine film of gold over a surface. Real gold leaf comes in the form of 'leaves' in a booklet and covers a gesso-treated surface best. Gold leaf is so fine that its final colour can be affected by the colour of the surface beneath it. Traditionally, therefore, before applying the gold leaf, the gesso base is given a coat of red bole, a red clay pigment that gives a rich, warm look to the gold finish.

There are two main methods of gilding with real gold leaf: water gilding and oil gilding.

Water Gilding

Used to achieve a high-gloss finish, ideally, you should be taught this method by a professional and even then a great deal of practice is needed to attain perfection. However, it is still a fruitful field for experiment by the more determined home framer.

Gesso and bole are applied to the wooden frame, which is then coated with water, and, finally, gold leaf. The leaf is then burnished to achieve the

Rabbit skin glue
Gesso can be bought ready-made, but if you want to make your own you must first bind the gesso powder by mixing it with rabbit skin glue. The glue is bought in granules or sheets and should be soaked in water overnight. Mix one part soaked glue to nine parts cold water, and gently heat the mixture in a double boiler. Add the gesso powder, usually referred to as gilders' whiting, until it has a creamy white consistency. Sieve out any lumps or strain through muslin.

1

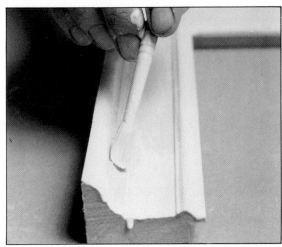

3

2

Applying gesso
1 First seal the wooden frame with a weak solution of rabbit skin glue and water.
2 Apply the first coat of gesso.
3 As soon as this has dried, rub it down with fine sandpaper, or wet and dry. To build up a smooth gesso base, repeat this procedure up to six times.

Building up gesso

1 *When the final coat of gesso has dried, rub it down to an extremely fine finish with wet and dry. At this stage you can actually wet the wet and dry. (Had you tried this at an earlier stage it would have dissolved the gesso and taken you back to the bare wood.)*

2 *Use a sculpting tool to remove excess build up of gesso in the corners of the frame.*

3 *The gesso coat should be perfectly smooth before adding the final finish.*

1

2

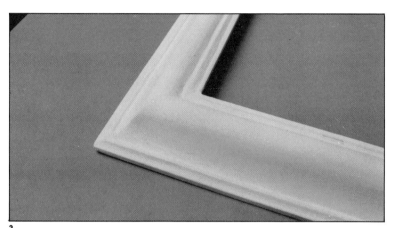

3

Applying bole

Before gilding, apply two or three coats of bole (left). Apply the first coat very thinly (below). Allow each coat to dry before rubbing down with fine sandpaper.

classic shine associated with gilded frames.

First apply the coats of hard gloss, that is, gesso that has been mixed with a large amount of glue to a hard consistency: two coats of hard gesso are usually sufficient. Then apply up to four coats of soft gesso, and sandpaper or glass-paper them finely. Now apply up to four coats of bole and rub down the surface with glass-paper to achieve an absolutely smooth finish. With a soft mop brush apply water containing a small amount of gelatine or methylated spirits and then place the gold leaf in position straight away. Finally, burnish the leaf, using a gilders' burnisher. If the burnisher cannot reach the small indentations in the more intricately moulded or carved frames, leave them matt; this adds to the richness of the finish by producing a variety of tone.

Oil Gilding

For oil gilding there is no need to apply the first coats of hard gesso and you can brush an ordinary coat of paint instead of the bole directly onto the gesso, ignoring the colour aspect altogether.

Oil gilding requires a non-absorbent surface and a coating of shellac glue is required to completely seal the surface. If you do not wish to use bole but do wish to achieve something of the earth-red colour which is such a good base for gold leaf, red colourant can be added to the shellac glue before it is applied. Ordinary red oil paint can also be used in this way. For silver leaf, black or yellow ochre are good colours to use for the base instead of red.

The surface must be slightly sticky before applying the sheets of gold leaf. This is achieved by coating the surface with gold size, a mixture of oil varnish and a drying agent, designed to provide exactly the right degree of 'tackiness', and obtainable from picture framers' supply shops.

SIMPLE GILDING

The alternatives to real gold leaf do not provide such an effective gilded finish but they are less expensive and simpler to apply.

Transfer Gold Leaf

All that is needed prior to positioning the transfer is to give the gessoed frame a coat of thin Venetian red acrylic paint. Then simply lay the transfer gold leaf on the surface and rub over it firmly with your fingers before stripping off the backing.

Metallic Powders

Apply straight onto the tacky surface; again a ground colour is desirable to give a rich sheen. Metallic powders are not suitable for large areas as they tend to took thin and insubstantial. After applying a powder, a coat of varnish is necessary to prevent it from being rubbed off the surface.

Wax Gilding

Again, there is no need for either gesso or bole. Simply apply an undercoat of paint to the wooden frame. Then make your own 'gilt' by mixing wax with metallic powder and rub this over the completely dry painting frame. Polish with a soft rag.

Gold or Silver Paint

Paint cannot usually be used to create the impression of gilding, although it can be useful occasionally for touching up small areas of gilding.

Wax gilding
Mixed wax and metallic powder is applied with a brush over an orange undercoat (left). It can also be applied with the finger (below). The proportion of wax to powder depends on the density of the metal finish required. Pre-mixed metallic wax is also available.

THE BASICS OF FRAMING

Transfer gilding

Before applying transfer gilding, make sure that the surface has been coated with gold size. It is important that this has dried to the right degree of tackiness to ensure that the gold adheres properly to the surface. Different types have different setting times, so follow the manufacturers' instructions.

1 Transfer gold comes in sheets on a paper backing.
2 Position a sheet on the frame.
3,4 Press it down lightly with the finger. Use a tool if you have to push it into a grooved molding.

5 Carefully remove the paper backing. Repeat this procedure until the required area is covered. Traditionally, red-brown bole is used as a base for gold, and black bole for silver. After applying the transfer gold, protect it with a coat of lacquer.

1

2

3

4

5

Water gilding

You will need a gilders' pad and knife, a badger brush and a thin solution of rabbit skin glue and water.

1 *Cut the gold leaf on the pad with the knife to the required size. This requires practice, as the leaf is very flimsy and tends to waft in the slightest draught.*

2 *Create static on a badger brush by rubbing it gently on the skin or hair, and pick up the leaf with it.*

3 *Place the water solution carefully on the area to be gilded, and brush into place.*

4 *The framer has used red lacquer to complete the design.*

1

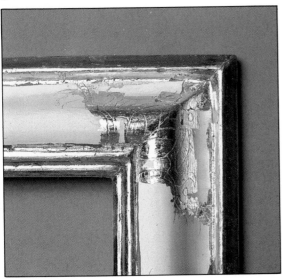

2

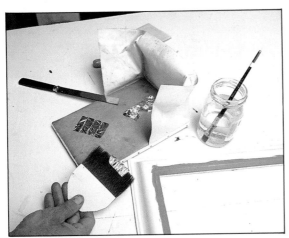

3

4

STAINING

Staining enhances rather than hides the natural patterns of the wood grain. Hardwoods take the stain particulary well, as their close-grained nature aids the even application of the dye. Softwoods are not so suitable for staining and should be well sanded beforehand.

Many colours of wood dye are available and they can be mixed to give further subtle shades. Stains used to be restricted to the more natural-looking colours but nowadays bright colours, too, are available.

Stains can be oil based or water based and care should be taken not to mix the two. Wood dye can be evenly spread with a soft brush, although it is often best to apply the dye with very fine steel wool, using rubber gloves to protect your hands. It is often easier to dye the separate pieces of moulding before assembling the frame. Rub the wood with turpentine before staining to remove any oil or grease marks.

WAXING

Natural or stained wood should be sealed to preserve its colour. The most natural-looking method of achieving this is to use wax. After the wood has been lightly rubbed down with a fine sandpaper, apply white polish, beeswax or ordinary household wax polish. Then buff the wax to give a sheen.

VARNISHING

A varnish provides a tough, hard-wearing finish but never gives quite the same professional look as wax

Antiquing silver transfer leaf
A silver transfer leaf frame can be antiqued with black staining wax—the type used on furniture. Rub it in with a rag, wait a few minutes, and then buff it up lightly to achieve a polished finish.

The same treatment can be used effectively on other finishes, including watercolour or gouache.

or polish. Varnishes are available in gloss, matt or semi-gloss; the high-gloss varnishes, however, can look shiny and synthetic and are probably best suited to bright and modern subjects.

ANTIQUE GLAZING

One way to give a frame an older look is to coat the frame with a subdued coloured glaze. This can be done over a plain colour or over a decorative painted effect.

Antique glaze can be purchased ready-made but it is simple to make: just add linseed oil, turpentine or white spirit and a drying agent to the oil colour chosen. Artists' oil paints provide a wide choice of colours, and earth pigments, such as raw or burnt umber or raw sienna, are popular because of their natural mature look but if you are antiquing a metal surface, plain black functions well as the basic glaze colour.

When you have mixed the glaze, apply it evenly over the frame: the brush should follow the direction of the wood grain. Then wipe off the glaze with a cloth, taking care not to wipe it away completely but to leave traces in the cracks and corners. This can be made permanent by giving the frame a coat of varnish when it is dry.

Oil-based glazes take a long time to dry, possibly a few days. Water-based tinted washes dry more quickly and can be made easily: tint very thin emulsion with watercolour or acrylic paint.

ANTIQUE SPATTERING

Antique spattering produces a freckled, mature look. The neutral colours that are used with glazes are best suited to this technique, although greys and black can alsolook attractive; use an antique glaze or Indian ink. Spattering can also be effective in toning down a too-bright under-colour.

Dip the stiff bristles of a brush into the glaze, paint or ink and spatter it unevenly over the frame by drawing your thumb over the top of the brush so that tiny spots of paint are flicked onto the surface. If the spatter is applied too evenly it looks like a mechanical paint finish, so make sure to keep the pattern random. If the finished effect looks rather stark, rub it down with a little steel wool when it is dry.

When the spattered frame is dry, add a coat of varnish to protect it. A high-gloss finish is not suitable for a frame that you wish to look old, so use matt or semi-matt varnish.

APPLYING FLAT PAINTS

Acrylic paints give a quick-drying and convenient basic coat, which can be left plain or waxed, or can be varnished or embellished with oil- or water-based paints.

Acrylics allow you to begin with a grey or neutral tone to which you can add subtle shades of a brighter colour to give a slightly warmer or cooler effect. To achieve this, mix a little of the colour to the grey

Scumbling
Apply a flat, oil-based undercoat. Here light grey is being used with brown and blue mottling. You can work with bought scumble glaze or make your own from artists' oil paint, linseed oil and turpentine. Using the lightest glaze and a soft bristle brush, stipple the surface in order to achieve an even but broken colour (left). Then apply a darker tone of scumble with a smaller brush (below left), aiming for a linear, veined effect. The finished frame is shown beside a darker version made with a dark grey undercoat and a light scumble glaze (below right).

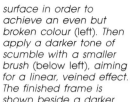

acrylic base and apply it as one coat; or apply a coat of flat grey acrylic paint and, after it has dried, apply a top coat of very diluted paint so that the grey shows through a translucent layer of colour.

Oil-based paints can also be used as finishes but take longer to dry. Modern high-gloss or 'wet-look' paints are more suited to a modern picture or frame. They are most effective as a finish when used with a light undercoat or gesso surface, which is lightly sanded. If gesso is not being used, coat the wood with wood primer before applying an oil-based paint.

Spray paints and enamels give a really professional-looking finish, free of any tell-tale brush marks around the mitred corners. They are particularly effective when applied to a surface that has been primed with gesso. They can be applied directly onto a well-sanded base of acrylic or latex emulsion but should not be used on an oil-based undercoat.

SCUMBLING

Best suited to plain, flat, angular frames, scumbling is a quicker way of achieving a marbling effect, although it does not have the same quality of finish. It consists of a flat undercoat, with more than one tone of scumble glaze on top applied with a circular motion of the brush. Mix scumble glaze from artists' oil paint, linseed oil and turpentine — to give it its 'glaze' or transparent quality. Alternatively, buy it ready-made in a variety of colours.

MARBLING

Like tortoiseshelling, marbling is done not to deceive the eye into thinking that it is seeing real marble but to produce a beautiful pattern based on the subtle markings of marble — it is a visual association rather than an exact replica. Again, it is a technique suited to plain, flat, angular frames rather than ornate mouldings, on which it would be impossible to create this style because of the number of ridges.

Paint an all-over glaze, made from white spirit and artists' oil paint, over the surface. Paint the veins of the marbling pattern onto this in short, jerky strokes, rolling and flicking the brush to give an impression of the actual seams in the stone. Before the veins are dry, blur them very thoroughly with a dry brush. Then go over it again, using the same colours and painting a few better defined veins onto the blurred background. This is surprisingly simple and effective and, providing that you use fairly

1

2

3

Marbling
1 *Starting with a cream ground, apply a loose ochre glaze. Use a smaller brush to rough in veins of dark brown.*
2 *Ruffle and blend the wet surface with crumpled newspaper. Soften the surface with a dry brush.*
3 *With a small artists' brush, add veins in blue and sepia glaze. Soften these with a broad brush or a feather.*
4 *Apply unsoftened, fine white veins with the tip of the feather to cross the existing pattern.*

4

Types of marble
Terra verde or green marble (above left) is made by applying green and white glazes over a black base. White marble (centre left) is created by painting thin black and grey veins over a white base. Golden marble (below left) is built up from ochre, sepia, blue and white glazes over cream.

Pattern and texture

1 *The framer is applying his own mixture of wax and black stain with a cloth to create a pattern.*
2 *A motif has been etched into the gesso base and decorated with a water-based paint and gold wax.*
3 *This frame was made from a piece of flat timber, which was coated with gesso and decorated with gold leaf and blue lacquer.*
4 *In this frame, a dark blue lacquer and gold motifs were used in a similar way.*

1

3

2

4

neutral colours without too much tonal contrast, it will produce a fine marble effect that will not intrude too much upon the picture.

TEXTURING

A textured finish is best suited to simple frames. A texture can be scratched into a paint surface to soften the effects of an austere frame without detracting from its simplicity. The traditional craftsman's method is to scratch or carve out a pattern on a gesso ground. A more practical and quicker way is to use a vinyl paint as the base.

Apply a thick coat of vinyl paint to the frame and texture it when the paint is partially dry so that it will be stiff enough to hold its shape and preserve the patterns you make. A simple, linear texture effected with a metal comb, a stiff brush or any other sharp implement can make an intriguing textured surface, turning a commonplace frame into an unusual one. Once you have created the textured surface, paint it any colour you wish.

WOOD – GRAINING

Wood-graining is a traditional technique, the object of which is not to produce a finish that looks exactly like wood but to produce a frank replica of a wood-grain pattern with paint. A coat of paint is applied, a glaze added and then wood-grain marks made on this. It is not necessary to confine yourself to

'woody' colours — some of the most exciting modern grain has been created in colours which were never seen in any natural habitat.

Start off by applying a coat of flat colour. This should be lighter than the glaze and, ideally, there should not be too much contrast between the two as the effect will be too stark. Use ordinary under-coat, or matt or eggshell emulsion for the first coat; gloss and enamel paints should not be used.

You can either buy the glaze and then tint it with a stainer — a strong, transparent liquid colour — or you can make your own, using the same method as for making antiquing glaze but with any colour. Brush a thin glaze of colour over the dry, under-coated surface, using a small decorator's brush, about the size of one normally used to paint a window-frame.

While the glaze is still wet, drag a brush with slightly spaced bristles across the surface to create hair-like streaks. Now flick a special grainers' brush — a soft brush known as a 'flogger' and available from specialist art shops — evenly over the surface to give a blurred effect.

TORTOISESHELLING

Tortoiseshelling gives a frame a luxurious finish, creating an unusual and special-looking effect. Care should be taken, however, not to overdo it because tortoiseshelling is essentially a paint finish

Wood–graining
There are two methods of wood-graining. In the first (right), medium oak scumble glaze applied on top of a pale, wood-coloured undercoat. Both are specially available for wood-graining. While the glaze is wet, it is combed with a rubber comb. The combed ridges are then smoothed out diagonally with a soft brush to create a softer line. In the second (far right, above), a paint glaze is brushed on freely and combed. Knots are touched in with a fingertip and then strengthened with an artists' brush. In the third method (far right, below), a soft dragger is used to create a mahogany pattern in wet, red-brown paint.

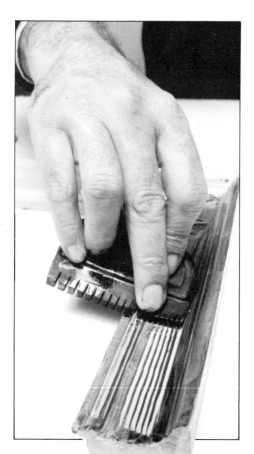

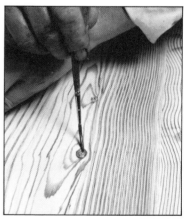

Golden tortoiseshell
1 *On a cream undercoat, apply tinted varnish in short, irregular strokes. Indian red blobs are also put on with a small decorators' brush.*
2 *Blend these in long, smooth strokes.*
3 *Apply blobs of Indian red and burnt sienna and work these in lightly with an artists' brush.*
4 *Blend these with a swift, crossing stroke. Finally, soften the whole surface by criss-crossing lightly with a wide, dry brush.*

1

2

3

4

— a frankly fake, exotic production, which can look overwhelming if it covers a very large area.

The tortoiseshell pattern is based on the polished pieces of tortoiseshell that show the internal seams of organic growth and feature them as a pattern. Originally, tortoiseshelling was applied mainly to small articles, such as combs, hairbrushes and dressing table mirrors, but it is now a popular paint finish for many surfaces, especially the surfaces of small items of furniture and picture frames. Study the style carefully and decide which of the varieties you require. They range from very dark to what is often referred to as blond tortoiseshell and the finished effect can be of blobs of spreading colour or, alternatively, of streaks.

The darkest styles of tortoiseshelling include one which is very distinctive and rich-looking. It was used

a great deal on Colonial-style furniture and is usually recognizable by its bold, dark streaks — often black or bronze — running over a mellow red background. Blond tortoiseshelling is effected over a light-coloured background, which may be metallic — using gold or silver. Fawn or light brown is usually used for the streaks.

Use a smooth, oil-based paint for the initial ground on which the pattern is to be based. The ground colour should be of a lighter tone than that of the required finish because the varnish and streaks will darken it. The key to successful tortoiseshelling is to work the design into the varnish while it is still wet, spreading successive layers of paint into patterns by lightly brushing diagonally in opposite directions with a dry brush. Use oil-based paints, such as artists' oil colours, for the streaks.

The Practice of Framing

1

MAN RAY

2

3

4

5

6

ROSE COTTAGE

7

8

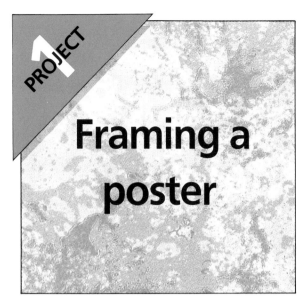

PROJECT 1

Framing a poster

This is a simple project—a poster is clipped beneath a sheet of glass, which can be purchased ready-cut, to an ordinary piece of chipboard. However, deterioration will develop unless steps are taken to strengthen this heavy artpiece and to preserve the poster from damage due to contact with the chipboard. To overcome these problems, a backing is provided for the poster and wooden battens are fixed to the edges of the chipboard. Screw clips can then be fixed to the battens rather than the chipboard, which is not really suitable for this, making the artpiece more secure and, at the same time, giving a more professional look to the piece.

Materials and Equipment

Poster	Small panel pins
Wooden batten, 6mm ($\frac{1}{4}$in) wide	Cardboard
Chipboard	Clips
Ruler	Bradawl
Craft knife	Short screws, 9mm ($\frac{3}{8}$in) long
Pencil	Cut and smoothed glass, 2mm ($\frac{1}{2}$in) or 3mm ($\frac{1}{8}$in) thick
Tenon saw	
Mitre box	
Hammer	Screwdriver
Resin glue	Screw-eyes or D-rings
Regular panel pins	Strong wire or cord

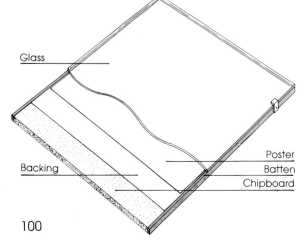

Glass

Backing

Poster
Batten
Chipboard

1 Select a length of wooden batten, 6mm ($\frac{1}{4}$in) wide, and a piece of ordinary chipboard. Measure the post to be framed and cut the chipboard to the same size minus 12mm ($\frac{1}{2}$in) in both height and width to account for the width of the batten.

2 Cut each piece of batten to a length which is 12mm ($\frac{1}{2}$in) longer than the corresponding side of chipboard. Then, using a mitre box, cut the corners of the frame in the battens. Using ordinary resin glue, fix the battens around the edges of the chipboard and nail them together with panel pins.

3 Glue and nail a piece of batten across the back of the chipboard, using small, 12mm ($\frac{1}{2}$in) panel pins to avoid penetrating the front of the board. It is from this batten that the artpiece will be hung on the wall, so place it one third of the way down from the top of the chipboard to hide the hanging-wire.

4 From cardboard, cut a piece of backing to the size of the poster. This will be placed between the poster and the chipboard to prevent damage being caused to the poster by the rough texture of the chipboard. The backing also lends a firmness to the final fitting and presents a smooth resting place for the poster.

5 You are now ready to fix glass, poster, backing and chipboard with clips. Sprung-steel emu clips are simple and popular but, for extra strength, a hardware or brass-fitting store can supply clips of the type shown here in brass, stainless steel, or the less noticeable Perspex, which we have chosen.

6 Position each clip carefully. Place two clips on the top, two on the bottom, and three on each side to hold the poster and glass securely. Make sure the clips are a few inches away from the corners and are neatly opposite each other. Their positions can now be marked with a bradawl.

7 To make holes for the screws that will fix the clips, hold the bradawl firmly but do not push and twist too hard. Only small holes need be made, as the best type of screw for fixing clips is a short, 9mm ($^3/_8$in) one.

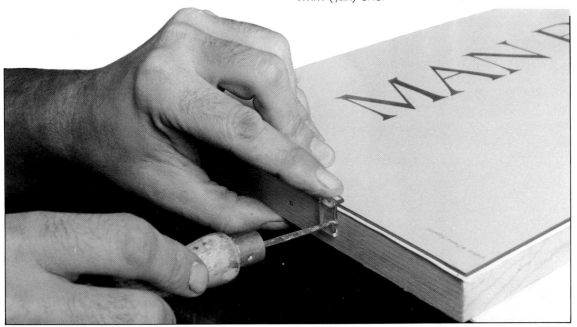

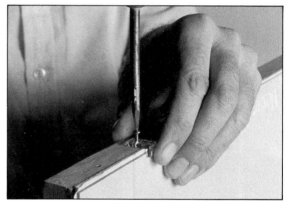

8 The component parts are now ready for assembling. Place the chipboard on a flat surface. Lay the backing board on top, then the poster, and finally the glass. Purchase glass either 2mm(^{1}/$_{12}$in) or 3mm (^{1}/$_8$in) thick but avoid anything thicker. Ask the glazier to smooth off the edges, or smooth them yourself with fine glass-paper.

9 Screw the clips into the wooden battens round the edges of the chipboard, using a small screwdriver. You will probably find it easiest to start the screws while the assembled poster and board are lying flat on the work-table. They can then be finished firmly, with the poster upright if necessary.

10 Lay the framed poster face down. Fasten two screw-eyes, or D-rings, to the batten across the back of the chipboard. To make hanging easier, keep these spaced wide apart. Run a strong wire or cord through each eye and fasten it so that it is fairly taut; knot it firmly. You may find it better to use the wire or cord doubled.

MAN RAY

Alexandre Iolas

PROJECT 2

Framing a watercolour

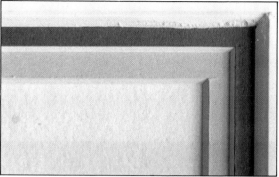

1 To frame this large watercolour, it was decided to use a deep, white mount, with two inner slip mounts, in colours matching those in the painting.

T he delicate lines and washes of a water-colour usually require a mount to set them off best. Moreover, watercolours are normally framed behind glass, which helps to preserve them, and the mount acts as a fixture to prevent the watercolour being pressed too tightly against the glass.

Materials and Equipment

Point-driver (optional)	Ruler
Nails	Hard, sharp pencil
Hammer	Craft knife or scalpel
Gummed tape	Thick, white mount card
Hardboard offcuts for corner pieces	Thin, coloured mount card
Bradawl	Aluminium-plated wooden moulding
Corner clamps	Saw
Screwdriver	Mitre box
Screw eyes for wall-hanging	Woodwork glue
Brass picture-frame wire	Heavy-duty cardboard
Pliers	Glass, 2mm (¹/₁₂in) thick

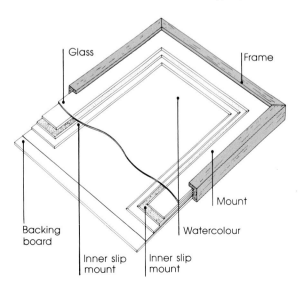

Glass — Frame — Mount — Watercolour — Inner slip mount — Inner slip mount — Backing board

2 Measure with even more care than usual when making slip mounts, as even a slight error is easily noticeable in a multi-mount. Slip mounts are usually the same width all round, while the outside mount is deeper at the bottom than on the other three sides to ensure that the picture sits up well in the frame. Cut the mounts and windows.

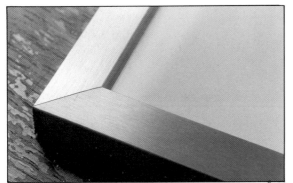

3 Measure the perimeter of the outer mount and cut a metal frame, mitring the corners in the usual way. You can obtain solid metal frames, which must be cut with a hacksaw, but the frame we chose was essentially wooden, with a coating of light aluminium, which enabled us to cut it with an ordinary saw. Glue the pieces together; do not nail the pieces in this case — nails would make the metal look untidy. Cut a piece of cardboard, measured to fit inside the frame, for the backing board.

5 Holding the machine down firmly on the backing board, pull the trigger and shoot a diamond-tack into the side of the frame. If you do not have a point-driver, tack the nails sideways into the inside of the frame.

6 It will now be necessary to stick the gummed tape to the edges of the backing board and the back of the frame to reinforce the structure and keep out the dust. Wet strips of ordinary gummed brown paper tape.

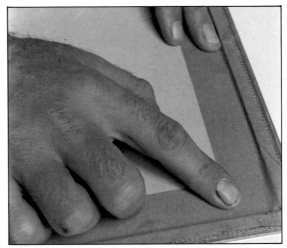

4 Turn the frame over and fit the pre-cut glass into the rebate. Next insert the triple mount, then the watercolour and finally the backing board. To hold this large frame together, a point-driver was used to tack the components together. Position the point-driver right up against the inside wooden part of the frame.

7 Press the tape into place, working slowly and carefully to ensure that no possible space is left for dust to enter. Take extra care when pressing the tape into the corners.

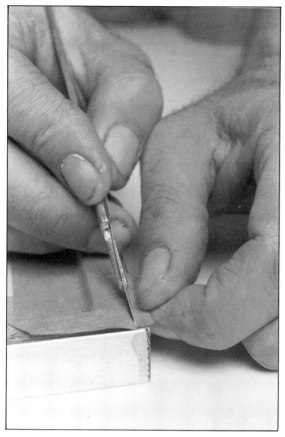

8 Trim off any excess tape with a scalpel. The back of the frame should now be thoroughly sealed. This is very important, as watercolours can be spoiled easily by dust and dirt.

9 To strengthen the corner joins, which were not nailed, as this is a metal frame, we made corner pieces from hardboard. You can also buy ready-made corner pieces in a variety of metals, if you wish.

10 The corner pieces are first glued and then nailed into place. Run strips of glue along the edges of the corner pieces. Try not to use too much glue as this might cause slippage.

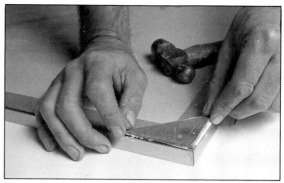

11 Place the corner pieces into position with extreme care; make sure they are not visible from the front of the frame. Glue into place, then wait for the glue to harden.

12 Using a bradawl, make holes in the back of the frame for nailing the corners. A steady hand pressure is essential to ensure that you do not damage the frame. Tap in the nails.

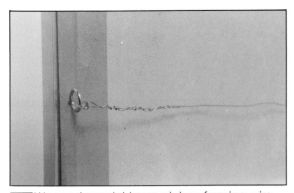

13 We used special brass picture-framing wire, obtainable from art shops, for this project, to bear the weight of the artpiece. Run the wire through one of the eyes and knot it. Tighten the knot with pliers and then wire and knot the other end, taking care not to leave the wire too taut. Wind the spare ends back around the wire.

14 A bradawl should be used to make holes in the back of the metal frame for hanging. Position the holes about a third of the way down the picture, one on either side, and screw in screw eyes.

15 The framing is now complete. Without dominating the picture, the slip mounts lead the eye into the watercolour and enhance the pale washes that were used in the painting.

PROJECT 3

Framing an oil painting

1 We chose pinewood, 50mm (2in) by 25mm (1in), generally available from builders' merchants, for the main frame. When measuring for oil painting frames, remember that the canvas on the stretcher is often slightly misshapen, so allow a tiny extra margin. After cutting and mitring, glue the corners and clamp them together.

This modern, dramatic oil painting stares boldly from the canvas. The wintry image is flat and graphic, and we therefore decided to use a deep box frame, painted a stark plain black to highlight the dramatic nature of the picture. We decided not to place the painting under glass; it is generally not necessary to glaze oil paintings.

Materials and equipment

Pine moulding, 50mm (2in) by 25mm (1in)	Tape
Hard, sharp pencil	Bradawl
Ruler	Punch
Saw	Fine surface filler
Mitre box	Sandpaper
Woodwork glue	Grey undercoat paint
Corner clamps	Black enamel spray paint
Corner clips (optional)	Paintbrush
Pliers	Steel tacks
Nails	Brass plate wall-fastenings
Hammer	Brass screws
Wooden quadrant	Screwdriver

2 This is a deep frame and the clamps are holding it firmly together at the bottom. However, there is no clamping pressure on the top and we used special sprung-steel clips to rectify this.

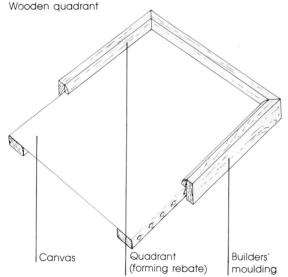

Canvas   Quadrant (forming rebate)   Builders' moulding

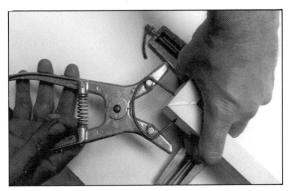

3 To fit the clips, special pliers are required to pull them apart. Position the pliers around the top of one corner, as shown, and release them, allowing the clip to spring into place.

4 Fit clips similarly on each corner, so that the frame is firmly held by clamps and clips. If you do not have special clips, tie string round the frame as a temporary measure. Then tap in nails to secure the corners, using a punch to tap them just below the surface.

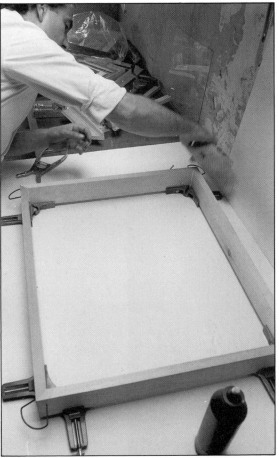

5 Allow the time specified by the manufacturer for the glue to dry, before releasing the clamps and clips.

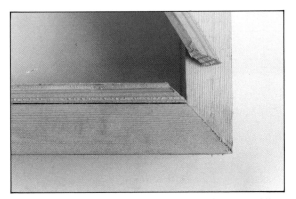

6 The wooden frame should fit snugly around the canvas. A rebate is now fitted to cover the edges of the canvas, giving a neater and more professional look and stopping the canvas from slipping out through the front. A wooden quadrant was chosen to make the rebate. Mitre the quadrant and place the strip onto the front of the frame, so that you can measure the lengths required. Mark off each corner and cut to size.

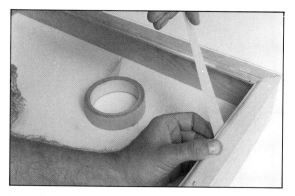

7 Glue the rebate strips into place. Bind strips of tape around the quadrant and frame to hold it in place, and wait for the glue to set.

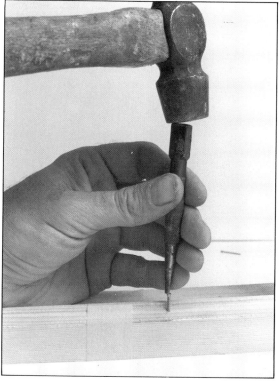

8 This solid, deep frame will stand upright without difficulty, and it is therefore easy to work holes into the quadrant and frame with a hand-held bradawl. Tap in the nails and sink them below the surface with a punch.

9 Fill in the nail holes with fine surface filler, obtainable from most hardware stores. At the same time fill in the holes made in the corners of the main frame. Then rub down the filler with sandpaper.

10 Brush a grey undercoat onto the completed frame, applying two coats. Sand this down. Then spray thinly with black enamel paint. Allow this to dry and then rub down gently with fine steel wool. Spray on several coats in this way, until you have achieved the finish you require.

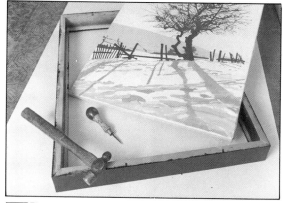

11 The components are now ready for assembly. You will need a bradawl, hammer and steel tacks. Make sure that you have a flat, uncluttered surface on which to lay the frame for final fitting.

12 Fit the canvas into the main frame, easing it up tight against the rebate. Check that it fits snugly before nailing. Then, using a hand-held bradawl, make the holes in the inside of the frame. Nail steel tacks sideways into the frame to hold the painting in place.

13 It was decided to fit the frame against the wall instead of hanging it and we selected brass plate fastenings for this, to be fitted to the sides of the frame. Position the plates so that they are exactly opposite each other and mark the holes with a bradawl. Screw on the plates with brass screws.

14 Screw the framed painting in place on the wall. It should sit flat against the wall to enhance the depth of the frame and give emphasis to the window effect of this landscape picture.

PROJECT 4

Framing a collection of photographs

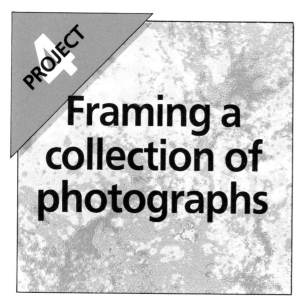

1 Arrange your photographs into a composition: ensure that none looks outwards or away from the group. In our collection, we had four photographs of the same size and one smaller one. It was decided to put the small one in the centre and range the others around it.

All the people in the photographs to be framed are from the same family, and all the photographs have a definite nineteenth-century flavour. They are therefore ideal candidates for a group mounting — all the photographs mounted within one large frame. By using a single mount with several windows cut into it, a backing board and glass — held in the rebate of a polished wooden frame that is enchanced by a gold slip — vitality and unity is given to what could easily be a collection of scattered photographs.

2 Use a piece of stiff cardboard — as here — or hardboard to provide a backing. For the mount itself, use mount card. Here, an ivory colour was chosen to give an off-white, subdued paleness, onto which decorative lines could be drawn.

Materials and Equipment

Stiff card or hardboard	Saw
Mount card	Middle oak woodstain
Sharp, hard pencil	Rag
Ruler with bevelled edge	Woodwork glue
Protractor or set square	Clear wax
Craft knife	Gold slip
Gummed paper	Glass, 2mm (¹/₁₂in) thick
Perspex ruler	Steel tacks, 25mm (1in)
Brown sepia ink	long
Gold ink	Hammer
Lining pen or felt-tipped	Screwdriver
pen	Brass screw eyes
Rebated moulding	Picture-frame wire
Mitre box	

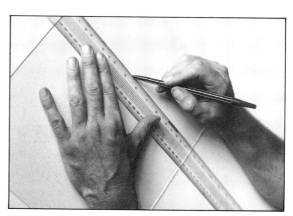

3 Backing board, mount and glass must all be the same size. If you wish to re-use an old frame, measure the height and width of the space within the frame, including the rebate overlap, while the frame is upside down, and cut the board, mount and glass so that they fit snugly into it. Otherwise, determine the size of the mount first, as we have done here, and then cut the frame and mount. Cut the board with a craft knife.

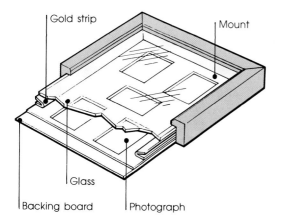

Gold strip — Mount

Glass

Backing board — Photograph

4 Decide where to place the photographs, using your own judgement, but leaving more space at the bottom of the photographs than at the top, so that they sit up high in the mount; we have placed the middle photograph with 150mm (6in) of space above it and 230mm (9in) of space below.

5 Measure each photograph. Subtract about 12mm (¹/₂in) from both the height and width measurements to allow for an overlapping margin of mount card — the photo will fit beneath the mount and must be slightly larger than the window, otherwise it will fall out. Lay the mount card flat and measure out the windows. If you are cutting by hand, rule lightly pencilled lines on the front of the mount card before cutting.

7 When cutting the windows, use a straight-edge with a bevelled slope and a rubber tread on the bottom to prevent it from slipping. Lay the straight-edge along the pencilled line on the front of the mount card. Place a craft-knife blade at the top of one line and score a light cut, holding the blade against the bevelled edge to give a sloped window. Run the blade along the line a second or third time until you have cut right through the card. Repeat this process until you have cut out all the windows.

6 Before cutting, check the right angles at the corners of the windows, using a protractor or set square.

8 Now stick down the photographs. Turn the mount card upside down and lay it flat. Place one photograph face downwards onto its window and stick a piece of tape along one edge of the back of the photograph. Then turn the mount card over to check that the photograph is correctly positioned.

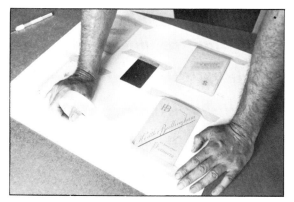

9 Once you are satisfied that the photograph is properly in place, turn the mount card face down again, and apply tape to the other sides of the photograph to secure it. Repeat this procedure with the other photographs.

11 Using an ordinary Perspex ruler, draw light lines with a sharp, hard pencil to mark where the decorative lines will fall. Check the right angles with a set square or protractor. It is up to you where you place the lines but avoid spacing them too evenly as this gives a dull effect. We decided to draw three lines around each photograph, one 6mm (1/4in) from the edge of the photograph, one 3mm (1/8in) beyond that and a third 15mm (5/8in) beyond that.

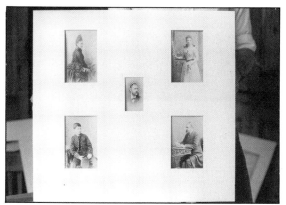

12 We used brown sepia ink for the two inner lines and gold ink for the outer one, drawing the lines with a lining pen. Place the rule upside down to avoid smudging the ink. Run the pen along the pencilled line slowly and continuously. Felt-tipped pens can also be used for the lines.

10 Make one final check with all the photographs in place. Notice the final effect, here, of placing the photographs so that they sit high up in the mount-space. The outside photographs have a 50mm (2in) space above them but a 75mm (3in) space below them; and they are arranged symmetrically, with a 12mm (1/2in) space between each, and a 75mm (3in) space between them and the middle photograph, and a uniform distance from the sides of the mount.

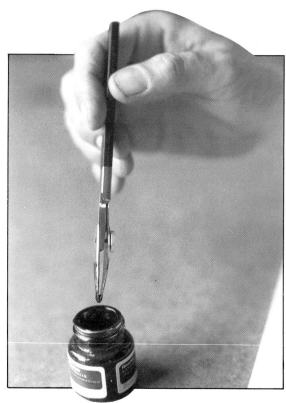

13 For the frame, we used a rebated frame moulding, cut into four pieces and mitred. Before joining, we stained the pieces with middle oak colour, using a rag to spread the stain. After joining, the frame was polished with clear wax.

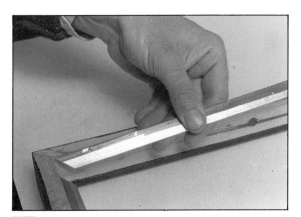

14 Lengths of gold slip add a final touch to the framing. Place a piece along the inside of the back of the frame and measure it by eye, marking it off so that it fits tightly into the rebate. Then mitre the pieces.

15 Turn the frame upside down. Fit the gold slip snugly into place into the rebate; next fit the glass; then the mount card with the photos; and finally the backing board. Tap 25mm (1in) steel tacks into the frame at an angle so that they hold everything in place against the rebate. There is no need to make holes first with a bradawl as the tacks are extremely sharp.

16 Tape the back along the edges with adhesive paper to keep out the dust. Finally, screw in two brass screw eyes into the back of the moulding, one on each side, a third of the way down the artpiece; run wire through from one side to the other and knot firmly.

PROJECT 5

Framing a manuscript

[1] Purchase a length of ordinary builders' moulding, or architrave, as it is also known. Professionals may cut a rebate into this with a plough plane but for this project a strip of quadrant was attached to the moulding to make a rebate.

Manuscripts usually have a serious, grey appearance. They can be brightened up considerably in the framing, without losing their dignity. We decided to use a triple mount for this manuscript, with a red slip included to give a touch of colour. We cut the mounts and windows first in the usual way.

[2] Glue the quadrant to the architrave. For extra strength, nail the two pieces together. Cut the finished length into four pieces and mitre in the normal way.

Materials and equipment

Mount card (red and two tones of grey)	Mitre box
	Saw
Hard, sharp pencil	Panel pins, 25mm (1in) long
Ruler	
Scalpel or craft knife	Pigments and shellac
Pine builders' moulding	Pewter wax
Quadrant	Polishing rag
Woodwork glue	Gummed paper
Nails	Bradawl
Hammer	Screw eyes
General purpose brush	Wire for wall-hanging
Vice or corner clamps	Pliers

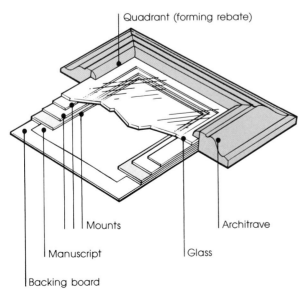

Quadrant (forming rebate)

Mounts

Architrave

Manuscript

Glass

Backing board

3 As an alternative to corner clamps, a vice can be used for making a main frame. Place one piece of quadrant and architrave firmly in the vice, and apply glue to the end.

5 Check that the glued pieces are held firmly in the vice before nailing the corners. Then hammer in a 25mm (1in) panel pin. One pin in each corner should suffice.

4 Adjust the vice to hold another piece against the glued strip. Make a hole ready for a nail, using a bradawl. Hand-held pressure is enough, as this is a piece of soft pine.

7 We applied a blue-black undercoat, using pigment mixed with shellac. We left a groove in this darker colour to add decorative interest and gave the rest of the frame a pewter wax finish. Ready-made waxes are available in different colours. Apply either with a brush or with the finger. Wait for a few days before polishing, or you will rub off the wax.

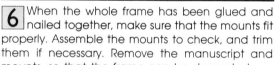

6 When the whole frame has been glued and nailed together, make sure that the mounts fit properly. Assemble the mounts to check, and trim them if necessary. Remove the manuscript and mounts, so that the frame can be decorated.

8 Assemble the glass, mount, manuscript and backing board and tap nails into the inside edges of the frame to hold the component parts together. Place gummed paper on the back to keep out the dust and attach screw eyes and wire in the usual way for hanging.

PROJECT 6

Framing a piece of needlework

1 A length of moulding is used for the inner, velvet-covered insert, or slip frame. Make sure that the rebate is deeper than the depth of the stretcher, so that the stretcher will eventually fit right down into the slip frame. Cut and mitre the wood, then spray the pieces with fabric glue.

Needlework is often attached to a stretcher before being framed to give it an extra smartness and tautness. Place the needlework over a stretcher similar to that used for an oil painting, and staple it round the edges.

We framed this piece of embroidery under glass, and it was decided to keep it from contact with the glass in an elegant way by putting a velvet slip frame between the embroidery and the glass.

Materials and equipment

Battens for stretcher
Hammer
Stapler for stretcher
Moulding with rebate
Hard, sharp pencil
Ruler
Mitre box
Saw
Fabric glue
Velvet
Scalpel or craft knife
Mahogany moulding with rebate

Woodwork glue
Elwood clamp or corner clamps
Glass, 2mm (¹/₁₂in) thick
Bradawl
Nails
Panel pins
Screw eyes for wall-hanging
Wire for wall-hanging

Embroidery on stretcher

Main frame

Velvet-covered slip frame

Glass

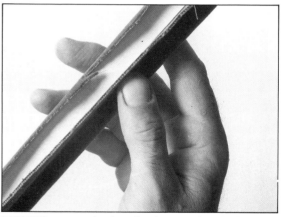

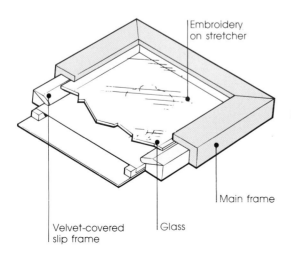

2 With a scalpel cut pieces of velvet large enough to cover the rebate, and front and side of the insert. Wrap each piece of velvet round a glued piece of insert and press home firmly.

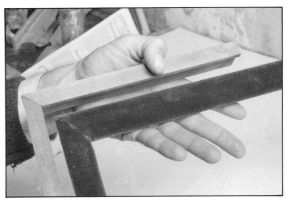

4 A length of mahogany moulding was chosen for the main frame. This outer frame, of course, must be deeper than the insert. Cut and mitre the moulding so that the insert will fit snugly into the frame.

5 We used an Elwood clamp for the frame. This clamp consists of four metal corners. The fourth corner has a screw-tightener attached to it and a piece of wire leading from it.

6 Apply glue to the mitred ends of the moulding, and stick together. Fit the corners of the Elwood clamp onto the corners of the frame and run the wire around the whole frame, making sure it sits in the grooves provided for it in the metal corners. Then fasten the wire in the screw-tightener and tighten it up just enough to ensure that the glued corners will be stuck firmly. Wait for the glue to dry and then nail the corners. Make the slip frame in the same way.

3 Make sure that the velvet covers the insert and rebate except at the back, so that only the velvet will show when the insert is fitted into the main frame. With a scalpel, trim off all the excess velvet from the edges and corners.

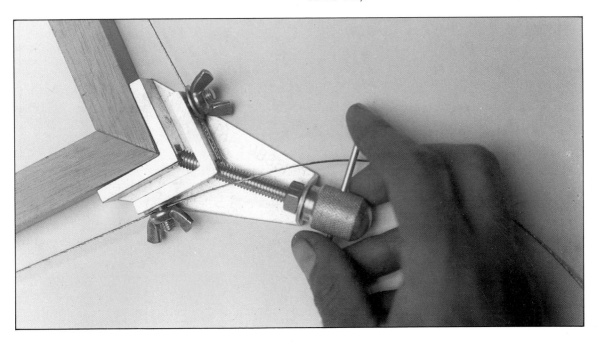

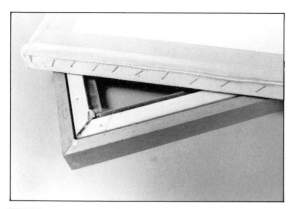

7 The components are now ready for assembly. Lay the main frame face down. Fit a piece of glass into its rebate and then fit the slip frame into the back of the main frame.

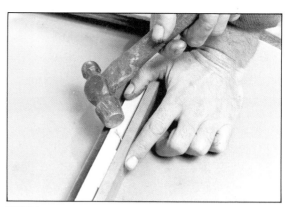

9 Hammer nails into the holes which you have made in the inside edges of the main frame. Use sharp panel pins to ensure that you can tap them into place without using too much force.

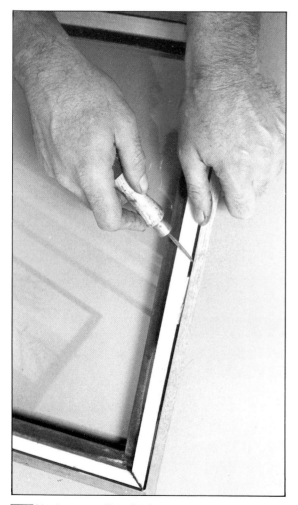

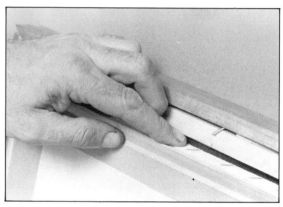

10 Now take the needlework on its stretcher and place it in the rebate of the slip frame. Tap nails into the inside edges of the slip frame to hold the stretcher in place.

11 The frame is now complete. The needlework is protected from dirt and dust by the glass, and protected from direct contact with the glass by the velvet-covered slip frame. A treasured piece of embroidery can be neatly preserved in this way.

8 Next, secure the slip frame in the outer frame. Make the holes in the outer main frame with a bradawl, one in each side. Remember that you will be doing this with the glass already in place and the slip frame behind it, so work in the bradawl gently.

Framing the three-dimensional

The butterflies to be framed were fixed with pins to cork bases, making framing a tricky, delicate affair. For instance, velvet was chosen for the background: should the cork bases be glued onto velvet? Glue could damage such a delicate material.

Black velvet was chosen to off-set the butterflies, an effect which could easily be ruined by dust. So a dust-free working environment was essential and care had to be taken to make the finished frame tight and secure.

Materials and Equipment

Box moulding, 50mm (2in) deep, 18mm (³/₄in) wide	Ruler
	Corner clamps
	Counter-sinker (optional)
Glass, 2mm (¹/₁₂in) thick	Bradawl
Sharp, hard pencil	Brass screws
Length of wooden quadrant	Screwdriver
	Black matt paint
Woodwork glue	Craft knife or scalpel
Hand drill	Black velvet
Panel pins, 15mm (⁵/₈in)	Hardboard
Hammer	Fabric glue
Punch	Screws, 15mm (⁵/₈in)
Dark woodstain	Gummed paper
Mitre box	Brass plates and screws
Saw	

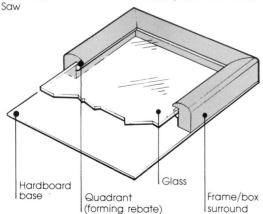

Hardboard base | Quadrant (forming rebate) | Glass | Frame/box surround

1 Choose a piece of moulding deep enough to ensure that a space large enough to accommodate the items to be framed exists between the glass and the back of the frame. We chose a piece of boxmoulding 50mm (2in) deep and 18mm (³/₄in) thick. Hold the glass along the edge of the rebate, and mark its precise thickness along the moulding with a pencil.

2 Select a piece of quadrant. This will be stuck along the inside of the rebate to create a groove in which the glass will be fitted. Make sure the quadrant is not so deep that it will be visible behind the glass.

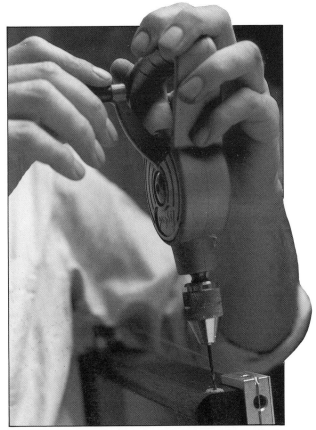

3 Place the length of quadrant along the moulding, and glue it in place over the pencilled line. Apply tape to give it extra temporary strength. Once the glue has set, drill small holes through the quadrant into the main frame and hammer 15mm (⁵⁄₈in) panel pins into it. Punch them beneath the wood surface for a neat effect.

6 The final side of the frame is not glued or nailed, but screwed on, so that it can be removed if the glass ever needs replacing. Holding the frame steady with a clamp, drill into the corners.

4 Stain the moulding and quadrant with a dark woodstain, and cut it into four pieces, mitring the corners in the usual way. Join two short sides and one long side of the frame to allow the glass to be fitted into the groove.

7 It is often a good idea to use a counter-sinker for fine-finish work of this type. By making tiny 'craters' at the entrance of the drilled holes, the screws will not jut out above the surface of the wood. Make sure you do not over-do this.

5 After glueing and nailing the three sides of the frame together, carefully slide the sheet of glass into place in the groove.

8 Carefully screw brass screws into the holes, resting them snugly in the hollow, to give a professional look.

11 Decide where you wish to place each specimen and measure out their positions on the back of the hardboard.

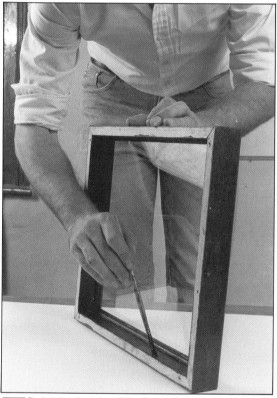

9 Paint the inside of the frame black. The use of a matt black will match, but not overwhelm, the black velvet that will provide a mounting base for the group of butterflies.

10 Measure out a piece of hardboard to the same size as the frame and stick the piece of black velvet onto it with fabric glue. Cut out the piece of hardboard.

12 As the slightest spilling of glue could damage the velvet, we decided to screw the cork bases in place in this project. This is why it was important to plot the positions of the butterflies on the back.

13 Using 15mm (⅝in) screws, carefully screw through the back of the hardboard, so that the screws protrude through the front. The cork bases of the butterflies are then carefully screwed onto the threads of the screws.

14 Place the hardboard and specimens onto the back of the frame. Make holes with a bradawl, drill and then fix a screw into each corner to provide a firm attachment.

15 Tape over the hardboard with gummed paper to make absolutely sure no dust can get in. Finally, fit brass plates to the sides of the frame so that it can be screwed flat onto a wall.

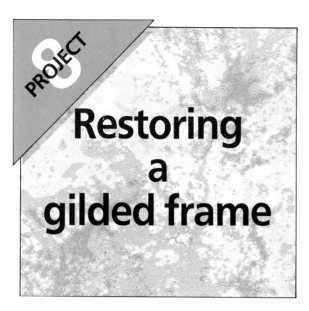

PROJECT 8

Restoring a gilded frame

1 Some of the ornamentation in this frame has cracked badly and some has been completely lost. There is extensive damage to one corner of the frame, and two sides need general repair.

This mid-nineteenth century wooden frame, gilded and beautifully embellished with intricate ornamentation, is sadly in need of repair. With skill and patience and some common materials, one of which is widely used by dentists, the frame can be brought back vividly to life.

2 Much can be achieved by cleaning with soap and water. Be careful not to use too much water as this can damage the frame. After cleaning off the surface grease and dust, lightly brush over with acetone, a chemical cleaner used for gold leaf.

Materials and equipment

Soap, water, rag
Acetone cleaner
Brush
Vaseline
Alginate mould solution
Knife (for spreading)
Cooking oil or grease
Plaster
Plaster spatula or carving tool

Woodwork glue
Sandpaper
Gesso
Bole
Gold leaf
Ormiline lacquer
Staining wax
Container such as a tin lid

3 In many cases, even the lost pieces can be 'recovered' by taking moulds from the good fragments that remain. Search the frame for areas of ornamentation still in good condition.

4 Apply Vaseline with a brush, working thoroughly into all the areas from which you intend to take moulds. This will prevent the moulding material from sticking to the wood.

6 While the mould is still in a semi-liquid state, apply it to the required spot. Press it into crevices and corners with a knife, working quickly, as it sets in a matter of minutes.

5 Mix the mould solution. Alginate, similar to the substance dentists use to make moulds for crowns, can be obtained from dental suppliers or from general mould suppliers, such as model shops. It gives a very high definition, and is very useful for moulding intricate embellishments.

7 Cover all the areas from which you intend to make moulds, and leave for a few minutes to allow it to dry and set. Apply a generous coating so that each mould will be strong and substantial when removed.

8 When they are set, peel the moulds off carefully. They will have a rubbery, flexible texture, but will tear quite easily. Also note that moulds made from alginate do not last very long.

9 Apply cooking oil or grease to the moulds so that the plaster will not stick to them. Select a plaster. Press the plaster paste into the mould and leave it for a few hours to set. Apply glue to the damaged areas and then press the plaster firmly into place, so that it blends with the surrounding ornamentation. Some minor alterations may need to be made; use a plaster spatula or carving tools for these finishing touches. Then rub down lightly with sandpaper.

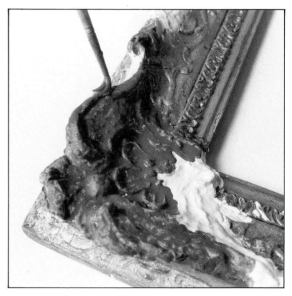

10 Apply two or three coats of gesso to the plaster to provide a base for the gold leaf. Rub down with fine sandpaper. Then apply two coats of bole colouring, a dark, terracotta reddish-brown, allowing time for drying in between applications.

11 Apply gold leaf in the usual way. Lacquer the gold leaf with ormiline lacquer, a hot colourless type, to provide protection. You will notice that the repaired sections of the frame look much newer than the rest of the frame. It is therefore necessary to tone down the new parts so that they blend with the rest. Waxes and pigments can be used for this.

13 Apply successive layers of wax with a rag, until the right colour is achieved. As an alternative to staining waxes, water and pigments can be used and then waxed afterwards.

12 Mix the staining wax and pigment in a shallow container; a tin lid is used here. A variety of waxes are available. We chose staining waxes with brown and black colouring.

14 You may have to work in several layers of wax before you are satisfied that the new areas blend with the original. The result will be a richly decorated frame, with the craftsmanship of an earlier era restored to perfection.

Care and repair

A central part of picture framing is the care and repair of the frames. Apart from looking after your own frames, you may wish to detach an attractive old frame from an unsuitable picture and give it a new lease of life. Or you may have an old print or picture that needs attention before it can be placed in a frame. Consequently, we have also included in this section some tips on simple picture cleaning and restoring.

If you do buy an old frame, first be careful to ensure that you are not spoiling a rare antique by attempting to renovate it. Your local antique shop should be able to advise you on this. If you have bought an old frame without antique value in itself, then you can achieve a great deal by cleaning and renovating it. For instance, if an old moulded plaster frame is damaged in places, it is usually well worth-while repairing these dents and chips by taking a mould from the good parts of the frame and using this to build up the damaged parts with filler. There are different ways of renovating gilding, from using

real gold leaf — if your frame is a particularly fine one — to simpler and quicker retouching. Sometimes it is just the glass which needs replacing and this is an easier task.

Although it is best to leave valuable works to the professional, there are some basic techniques which, once mastered, will enable you to carry out many minor repairs to give a surprisingly new look to pictures and frames.

REPAIRING OLD FRAMES

It is important to be cautious when renovating old frames and if in doubt give the job to a professional.

Most of the frames bought from antique shops are nineteenth- and early twentieth-century reproductions. While these are not particularly valuable, they are well-made frames, more individual and interesting then many modern mouldings, and well worth reviving, as they will probably last for many more years.

Many such frames have some kind of gold finish. Some are basic wooden frames with plaster mouldings and gilded finishes; others are carved wooden frames decorated in gold leaf; and others are gold-painted wooden frames.

When cleaning gold leaf, there is one important 'don't' to remember: never harshly rub or wash it with water, as this action wipes off much of the actual gold surface, a veneer so delicate that it is all too easy to damage. Instead, carefully wipe the gold leaf with a diluted bleach solution or acetone; or brighten the gold with lemon, rubbing a slice of lemon gently over the moulding.

Mending Chipped Gilt

The easiest way to mend small chips in gilt is to touch up the damaged spot with gilt paste, which is available in art and craft shops, or, if very small, with gold paint. However, if a small portion of the moulding is missing, it might be necessary to fill in the missing area with plastic wood, barbola paste, putty or

Replacing decorations
Badly damaged or chipped frames can often be repaired by making plaster replacements for the damaged parts from moulds taken from good portions of the frame. If a frame still has a good corner, for instance, a whole corner piece can be recreated in this way (right).

The gilded frames (left and below) are both slightly chipped. Such chips can be repaired by casting plaster replacements from moulds. Alternatively, very small areas can sometimes be built up by hand and touched up with gold paint. The gold slip frame (far left) is held in place by wooden wedges — a device often used in older frames.

Secondhand frames

This frame (right) was bought secondhand, in poor condition. The gesso and gilt were chipped and the corners were worn and loose. The frame was first thoroughly cleaned and then dismantled. The corners were then re-mitred, so that the frame fitted the new painting precisely.

Damaged frame
The gilded frame around this landscape print (right) *is faded and badly damaged. The chipped, damaged corners* (above) *could be touched up but in this case the framer decided to remove the gesso and gilt completely* *by soaking and scrubbing. Many such old frames have solid and attractive wooden bases that can be cleaned and polished.*

decorators' filler. Such a filler can be moulded into shape with a paintbrush handle or fine sculpting tool to blend it in with the original. When the area is dry, it can be matched to the original with the gilt paste.

Of course, gold leaf itself can be used to repair original gold leaf surfaces. However, this is rarely advisable as new gold leaf shines brightly and will look out of place on a more mellowed gold leaf frame. All gilt repairs tend to suffer to a certian extent from this problem but there are a few ways of getting round it. One way is to make use of the anti-quing technique described on page 92. Another is to age the new gilt instantly: rub tiny amounts of adhesive onto the newly renovated moulding and sprinkle a little dust onto the area. Wipe away the loose dust and you are left with a perfect older-looking frame.

Larger Repairs

If an area of wooden or plaster moulding is missing that is too large or too intricate to build up with filler materials, it is sometimes worth making your own mould for the missing portion. This is usually not too difficult as many of the frames requiring this treat-ment were themselves originally manufactured from moulds. *(See pages 128–131 for further details.)*

Use a piece of the frame which is intact and un-damaged as the base for your mould. Press Plasticine onto this area of the frame to obtain an impression of the pattern. Remove from the frame and build up the edges of the Plasticine mould with more Plasticine. Then pour in plaster of Paris up to the depth required to fit into the missing section.

When dry, remove the dried plaster moulding from the Plasticine and glue it into place.

Although Plasticine is easily available from department stores, many modern picture framers use alternative substances, such as silicone rubber and an organic material based on seaweed called Alginate, which can be obtained from specialist stores. The organic material and the silicone rubber give very precise impressions but Alginate lasts only a few days once the mould has been made, so is not suitable for long-term projects.

Stripping Old Frames

Some old plaster frames are beyond repair and may not be to your taste in any case. Do not throw these away, however, as most old plaster mouldings were created on very well made wooden bases, often pine, which make excellent frames in their own right. Remove the plaster by immersing the frames in hot water and scrubbing. When the stripped frame is dry, finely sandpaper it and then wax or stain it to produce a solid, new-look frame.

REPLACING GLASS

Often what seems to be a dingy or yellowed picture is in fact a clean picture languishing behind a dirty, ageing, nicotine-stained piece of old glass. Very old-fashioned glass often distorts a picture. Some-times the glass can be removed and washed; sometimes it needs replacing.

To dismantle a frame, place the picture face down on a clean, soft surface. Then gently remove the tacks which hold the backing and the picture in place. Lift up the picture and remove the glass.

Renovating oil paintings

Surface Dirt

It is a mistake to assume that your rather gloomy-looking oil painting is necessarily a dirty one. Many such paintings were intended to look dark: portraits and still-lifes, for instance, were traditionally given a dark background in the eighteenth and nineteenth centuries, and many landscape painters used a great deal of brown in their trees and grass. Many paintings look dark because of the mastic varnish covering them. This type of varnish, widely used until twenty years ago, has a dulling effect on paintings that is now familiar — the yellowing skies, brown foliage, and general dinginess often seen on pictures found in attics, junk shops and the more neglected museums.

However, many paintings are simply dirty and there are some basic steps which can be taken to improve them before reframing them. Surface dirt, accumulated through years of exposure to dust, nicotine, oil lamps and open fires is relatively easy to remove without damaging the picture (although it is not advisable to do even this much on a picture of high value). Wipe the surface of the old painting with cotton wool soaked in white spirit. The older the varnish, the safer this method is: if a picture has been varnished recently, the white spirit will tend to dissolve the varnish as well. By removing the surface grime in this way, the colours of the painting can be appreciably brightened.

You may find that a painting has not been varnished at all and that dirt is engrained into the paint. If this is the case you will need to wipe the painting with cotton wool soaked in a weak solution of ammonia to remove the dirt. However, by using ammonia you do run the risk of removing the paint as well as the dirt, so do not attempt it on any paintings that are valuable to you.

Removing Old Varnish

Extreme caution is required when removing a coat of old varnish from a painting. Tackle a small area at a time, using a solvent such as acetone, methyl alcohol or ethyl alcohol; if the varnish is fairly new, white spirit might be sufficient. Starting with the darker areas, apply the solvent cautiously with swabs of cotton wool. It is better to leave fragments of old varnish, which will not necessarily be noticed, than to be so anxious to remove every scrap of old varnish that you also remove a crucial detail of the painting.

Dealing with Flaking Paint

The professional will go to great lengths to recover flakes of paint that are missing from a painting. This is not so ridiculous as it sounds, especially if the painting has been behind glass, since the missing flakes will be stuck somewhere in the frame. Once discovered, the restorer will patiently fit the flakes back into the picture as though completing a jigsaw puzzle. The pieces are stuck into place with beeswax, which has a very low melting point. The beeswax is placed on the appropriate spot in the picture and the flake of paint positioned on top of this. Then a heated spatula — a very fine one — is applied on top of the flake, so that the beeswax beneath melts and the flake can be precisely manoeuvred into position. Although this is a specialist technique, there is no reason why the home renovator cannot become

adept at it, using a heated teaspoon handle instead of a spatula if need be.

If the missing flakes of paint are irretrievably lost and you do not wish to hand the painting over to an expert, you might wish to paint over the problem areas.

Sometimes, a fine portion of missing paint will have left an uneven picture surface. An indentation can be built up very carefully, using interior decorators' filler or even putty and, in the case of a very slight indentation, a thicker layer of paint may suffice.

Use either oils or acrylics to paint over the problem spots of the picture. These areas will often be white: where the top paint has flaked off, the white prime — the 'undercoat' which is applied to the canvas before the oil paint — usually remains. The advantage of using acrylic paint, especially if it is to be applied thickly, is that it dries very quickly; the equivalent amount of oil paint can sometimes take weeks to dry.

If you are not used to painting, remember that you must match the tone as well as the colour. For instance, a red jacket may not be red in the simple sense but might actually be a more dingy colour and contain more grey than red. It is advisable to tone down your colours with a neutral pigment, such as raw umber or Payne's grey, and experiment on a separate piece of paper until you obtain exactly the right shade.

Cracks in the Paint

Almost all old paintings have surface cracks, which actually serve to authenticate the picture. By studying the distance between the cracks and identifying the types of cracks that they are, an expert can 'read' a painting, that is, identify when the painting was originally executed. Experts suspect a fake if they can find no cracks, or if the signature contains no cracks, and if one area

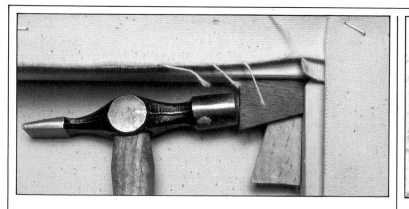

of a painting is without cracks it has probably been repaired.

Therefore, unless the cracks in your old oil painting are really disfiguring, it is best to leave them alone.

Revarnishing

Either matt or gloss varnish can be coated onto an old painting, although a very high-gloss varnish will look unnatural. Dilute the varnish to two parts varnish and one part white spirit and apply it with a brush vertically, then horizontally, using even, parallel strokes to achieve a smooth coat. Avoid applying thick coats of varnish as this will make the picture look as if it has been encapsulated in plastic.

Alternatively, use a spray can of varnish; this is preferable, as an aerosol gives a more even application than a brush. Nevertheless, the varnish must still be sprayed in thin, light coats: hold the picture upright and spray it from about 30cm (1ft) away, avoiding a build-up of varnish in any one area, which would probably drip.

Whichever method you use, it is absolutely essential that you work in clean, dust-free surroundings. If any particles of fluff or dirt become stuck in the varnish, they will look prominent and unsightly.

An old print

This print (right) is typical of many that you will come across. It is badly damaged and in need of flattening as well as cleaning.

Making the canvas taut
Purpose-built stretchers have corner wedges which can be tapped in gently (above). This pushes the sides apart and tightens the canvas.

Tightening the Canvas

Tightening a canvas that has become loose is a simple task. In many cases, professionally made canvases can be made taut again without having to remove the tacks that join the canvas to the stretcher. If you turn the canvas over, you will usually find that the corners of the stretcher have been slotted together and held slightly apart by tiny wedges of wood to provide the original final tightening of the canvas. A gentle tap will drive these wedges inwards slighly and provide a new tautness for the canvas.

Many prints and watercolours become damp over the years and, like oil paintings, their surface can become dingy with dust. Because prints and watercolours are usually executed on paper, they are also subject to staining, mildew and buckling. They can be ripped and scratched, too.

Removing Surface Dirt

Removing grime from a dingy surface, often the result of the print not having been behind glass, is not simply a case of giving the surface a quick wipe, as it can be sometimes with oil paintings. Because the paper on which the painting was done is porous, the grime will have been absorbed to a certain extent. Removing dirt from the picture surface, therefore, is a job for an expert. However, the white areas

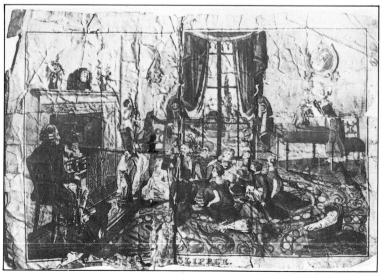

around and within the picture can sometimes be dealt with by the home renovator — and this can often be enough to give the whole picture a facelift. Wipe gently over the white areas with a putty rubber. Alternatively, wipe the whole surface with carbon tetrachloride — a dry-cleaning solution available from the chemist's. This must be wiped evenly all over the picture, including the image area, to avoid a blotchy result.

Dealing with Creases

Creases can sometimes be removed by sandwiching the canvas between two sheets of blotting paper and keeping it under a heavy, even weight for several days. If this does not work, it may be necessary to stretch the paper. Immerse the picture in cold water for just long enough to wet the paper (the water will not make the watercolours run as long as the whole print is immersed). Then place the picture on a flat surface and stick it down with brown paper tape. Allow the picture to dry naturally — artificial drying makes the paper contract too quickly and tear. Remove the tape to leave a completely flat picture.

Removing Damp Stains and Foxing

Damp stains and the little spots of mildew known as foxing can be removed by bleaching. Do not use ordinary commerical bleach; one per cent standardized sodium hypochlorite solution is suitable — the solution used for sterilizing babies' bottles, obtainable from chemists. Mix it in a ratio of one part solution to three parts cold water and put it into a flat photographers' tray or baking dish. Immerse the print or watercolour in the solution for a few minutes until the blemishes start to disappear. As soon as the dark spots begin to fade, remove the print and place it in a bath of water for a few minutes to wash away the bleaching solution. After rinsing, you may well need to stretch the canvas, especially if the watercolour is on light- to medium-weight paper. Partially dry the canvas naturally, then place it between two sheets of clean, dry blotting paper to finish off the drying. The marks should by now have disappeared.

Covering Scratches

Retouching a scratched area is generally a professional job. However, if you do decide to embark on this, begin with a paint that is more diluted than usual and gradually build up the

The problem of mould
This print (above) is marred by mould. Most engravings will withstand washing and, sometimes, bleaching. Here, an oxidizing agent will be used to remove the stains and improve overall appearance.

intensity of the colour. When repairing tears, it is important to lay the surfaces together without disturbing the fibres in the paper, which means that you must find their original positions and piece them back together before glueing them into place.

TEARS

Small tears, where there is sufficient overlap, can usually be repaired by applying acid-free, colourless adhesive that does not shrink as it dries. To repair large tears, however, you will probably need to fix thin backing paper to the back of the picture, so that no gap is visible.

Damaged engraving
Varnish, applied to give the appearance of an oil painting, has darkened with age on this hand-coloured print (left). A solvent was needed to remove ingrained varnish deposits.

Glossary

Abstract expressionism
An art form in which expression of the artist's inner experience is more important than realism. Paintings are created from involuntary marks and dribbles of paint.

Acrylic paint
A comparatively new paint in which the pigment is suspended in a synthetic resin.

Ancien Régime
The period in Europe before the French Revolution.

Architrave
The moulded wooden trim used around door and window frames.

Baroque
The richly decorative style of the post-Renaissance, prevalent in the seventeenth and eighteenth centuries.

Batten
Narrow strip of wood, sometimes used to frame an artpiece.

Bevel
The rounded or sloped edge of a ruler or strip of wood, or the sloped inside edge of a window in a mount.

Block mount
A block of wood or chipboard onto which a print or other picture is mounted.

Builders' moulding
Strips of wood used by builders for trimming doors, windows, skirting boards etc, which can be used to make picture frames.

Chipboard
Rigid board made from compressed chips of wood.

Clip frame
A simple frame without an edge or surround, formed by clipping a sheet of glass to a wooden backing.

Cold mounting
See Wet mounting.

Composition
The arrangement of the elements that make up the content of a picture.

Conservation mounting
Mounting carried out with acid-free materials to preserve old or valuable documents and pictures.

Damask
A fabric woven with a pattern which is visible on both sides.

Dry mounting
A method of sticking a picture onto a backing. A sheet of film is placed between the two and heat is applied. The film dissolves, fusing the picture and backing. Also known as hot mounting.

Emery
Cloth or paper covered with emery powder, for sanding a fine finish.

Empire style
The fashion associated with Napoleonic France, in the late eighteenth and early nineteenth centuries.

Foxing
Tiny spots of mildew that can form on old prints and drawings.

Framers' moulding
Strips of rebated wood especially designed for picture frames.

Fresco
Painting carried out on mortar or plaster that is not quite dry.

Gesso
Prepared surface of plaster as a ground for gilding and other finishes.

Gilding
Applying a gold finish.

Glaze
(1) To cover with glass, as with glass in a frame. (2) A thin coat of a transparent colour that is placed over a differently coloured undercoat.

Gold leaf
Thin sheets of beaten gold which can be applied to frames.

Hinge mount
A mount which opens and closes on a hinge, enabling the picture to be positioned and removed easily.

Hot mounting
See Dry mounting.

Insert
A smaller frame within the outer frame. Sometimes referred to as a slip frame.

Mastic
Natural gum from which some paints and varnishes are made.

Memorabilia
Articles and ephemera that have nostalgic associations.

Mitre
The 45-degree angled cut, made in the ends of each side of the frame.

Modernism
Art styles pertaining to and identifying with the twentieth century.

Mount
The card which is used as a backing for a flimsy picture, and the card from which a window is cut, beneath which a picture is placed.

Neoclassical revival
Art movements of the eighteenth and nineteenth centuries that looked back to classical, ie Greek and Roman, times.

Neutral
Without positive or distinctive characteristics.

Patina
A finish often used as a base for glazes or to modify and tone a colour.

Perspex
Tough, inflexible type of plastic available in sheet form and sometimes used in framing instead of glass.

Quadrant
Strip of wood or metal, shaped like a quarter-circle, often used to form a rebate.

Rebate
The L-shaped groove on the reverse side of framers' moulding into which the glass, mount, artpiece and backing board fit.

Sampler
Piece of embroidery worked in a variety of stitches, which was traditionally worked to demonstrate accomplishment in needlework.

Score
To cut, in glass or card, a line that does not pass through the material completely.

Sepia
A rich brown pigment obtained from cuttle fish. Now used to describe the colour only.

Slip frame
An inner frame, usually covered in fabric, inserted between the main frame and picture to provide a decorative border in the same way as a mount. Also known as an insert.

Stretcher
An expandable wooden frame to which a canvas is usually tacked before framing, so that it can be made taut in the frame.

Transfer gold or silver
Thin sheets of beaten gold or silver attached to paper and rubbed onto the surface of a frame.

Veneer
A thin layer or inlay of flat wood applied to a surface.

Vignette
A picture or design, usually done on a small scale, without a boundary.

Wash
Thinly diluted paint used to obtain a transparent or delicate paint finish.

Wet mounting
A method of sticking a picture to a backing, using spray glue or wallpaper size. Also known as cold mounting.

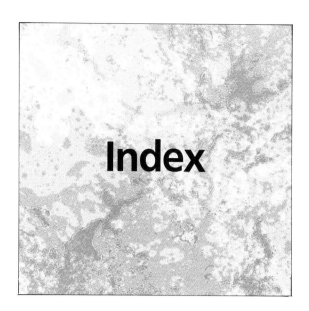

Index

Page numbers in *italic* refer to illustrations and captions

Acknowledgements

The pictures on these pages were produced by courtesy of the following:

8 Scrovegni, Padua; **9** National Gallery, London (t,b); **10** National Portrait Gallery, London; **11** Private collection, London; **14** Private collection, London (tr,br); **15** Private collection, London (t,b); **16** Private collection, London (bl,cr); **17** Private collection, London; **18** Private collection, London (t); **19** Private collection, London (r); **20** Private collection, London (tl,bl,br); **23** Private collection, London (t,b); **24** Elizabeth Whiting & Associates; **25** Elizabeth Whiting & Associates; **26** Elizabeth Whiting & Associates (tl,bl,tr,br); **27** Elizabeth Whiting & Associates (t,b); **28** Elizabeth Whiting & Associates; **29** Elizabeth Whiting & Associates (t); **31** Stan Smith (t), Rosie Waites (b); **34** *The World of Interiors*, photograph – John Cook; **35** Trustees of the British Museum, London (t); **39** *The World of Interiors*, photograph – John Cook; **40** Sandell Perkins Ltd, London; **42** *The World of Interiors*, photograph – John Cook; **43** *The World of Interiors*, photograph – John Cook; **136** Victoria and Albert Museum, London (br); **137** Victoria and Albert Museum, London (bl,tr).

With special thanks to Patricia Monahan and John Shrimpton.

All other photographs are the property of Quarto Publishing Ltd.

Key: (t) top; (b) bottom; (l) left; (r) right; (c) centre

While every effort has been made to acknowledge all copyright holders, we apologize if any omissions have been made.